I0424204

Hibiscus Masonic Review

Hibiscus Masonic Review

✦

Volume 1 / 2007

PUBLISHED BY

HIBISCUS LODGE NO. 275 CHARITABLE FOUNDATION

A CHARITABLE AND EDUCATIONAL FOUNDATION
SPONSORED BY

HIBISCUS LODGE NO. 275, F. & A. M.

CORAL GABLES, FLORIDA

HIBISCUS MASONIC REVIEW
VOLUME 1 / 2007

iUniverse books may be ordered through booksellers or by contacting:

iUniverse
1663 Liberty Drive
Bloomington, IN 47403
www.iuniverse.com
844-349-9409

ISBN: 978-0-5954-3054-3 (sc)
ISBN: 978-0-5956-8313-0 (hc)
ISBN: 978-0-5958-7396-8 (e)

Print information available on the last page.

iUniverse rev. date: 04/12/2021

Edited By Peter J. Millheiser, M.D., F.A.C.S.

For The Hibiscus Foundation
editor@hibiscuslodge.com

Front cover design by
Bros. Jean-Aimé Medici and Alfred Smith

Contents

EDITORIAL POLICY

The Hibiscus Masonic Review welcomes papers on Masonic history or culture. The papers should be original, embodying the personal work of the author and should be submitted to the editor in the English language either as a Microsoft Word © document sent by email attachment or printed in 12 point type, Times New Roman or Garamond font, and on white paper, one side, double-spaced with at least 1 inch margins on both sides. The papers should contain a bibliography and any photographs should be in black and white and should be at least 300 dpi.

The papers published in this journal may be read aloud in whole or in part in any Masonic Lodge, Chapter, Council, or other Masonic meeting without permission but it is requested that appropriate credit be given to the source and the specific author.

Questions, requests for copies of the Journal, or Papers should be submitted to the Editor, Peter J. Millheiser, P.M. at

editor@hibiscuslodge.com

or to

Editor
Hibiscus Masonic Journal
c/o Hibiscus Lodge No. 275, F. &. A. M.
P.O.B. 770218, Miami, FL, 33177–0004

www.hibiscuslodge.com

THE FOUNDERS OF HIBISCUS MASONIC REVIEW

Lynn Bauer
In memory of
W∴ Paul A. Bauer
W∴ Carlos E. Cespedes
Joseph I. Chi
W∴ David A. Cockrell
Stanley S. Davidson
Ainslee R. Ferdie
Ruben Garrote
W∴ John M. Holian
W∴ William W. Lansford
R∴ W∴ Joseph M. Martin
Jean-Aimé Medici
W∴ Peter J. Millheiser
Joe R. Poerschke
Theodore Sharon
W∴ William G. Staley
R∴ W∴ Steven Q. Steele
Stylianos G. Vayanos
Andres Venereo
Henry S. Waldman
Robert M. Wasserman

HIBISCUS LODGE, HIBISCUS FOUNDATION, AND THE HIBISCUS MASONIC REVIEW

Hibiscus Lodge was founded in Miami Beach, Florida in 1948. The name of the Lodge was selected because the hibiscus flower was the Florida flower most closely resembling the forget-me-not. The forget-me not was the flower worn in their lapels by Masons in Germany in the World War II period as a means of recognition and identification with the Craft subsequent to Hitler's closing of the Masonic Lodges in Germany prior to the war. By choosing this name, Hibiscus Lodge sought to identify with, as well as to memorialize, those Masons who suffered and even died under the oppressive hand of tyranny.

For more than forty years, Hibiscus Lodge was located in Miami Beach, Florida. It subsequently moved a few miles to the Coral Gables Masonic Temple. Today, Hibiscus Lodge is a very active Traditional Observance Lodge stressing brotherhood, spirituality, and education. Each new Mason is required to deliver a paper before the Brothers of the Lodge prior to advancing to his next Degree. This is frequently done at the Hibiscus Fellowship Club which was organized by the Brothers of Hibiscus Lodge for the purpose of recreating many of the features of the traditional ancient table lodge while serving as an informal venue for Masonic education. The Hibiscus Fellowship Club meetings are open to all Masons of the Degree of Entered Apprentice and above and are held several times yearly.

Hibiscus Lodge meets on the 2nd Tuesday of the month at the Coral Gables Masonic Temple at 41 Valencia Ave. in Coral Gables, Florida, with dinner at 6 PM and the meeting at 7:30 PM. On the 4th Tuesday of the month, there is typically either another Hibiscus Lodge meeting at the same time in the Lodge or a Fellowship Club meeting held in various locations.

The Hibiscus Lodge No. 275 Charitable Foundation is a charitable organization created by the Brothers of Hibiscus Lodge. The Foundation has funded a variety of local projects including university educational grants to disabled graduating high school students through its Tendrich Scholarships, as well as grants to many organizations including local schools for the purchase of musical instruments, for food for the needy, and to Shake-a-Leg Foundation for their many programs to bring independence and pleasure of life to people with significant disabilities.

As part of its educational focus, the Hibiscus Foundation is proud to sponsor the Hibiscus Masonic Review as an international forum on Masonic history and culture. The aim of this journal is to explore the many strands of intellectual thought that have contributed to the development of Freemasonry. The Review is under the direction of the Brothers of Hibiscus Lodge and has been created as part of its intensive educational program. Its aim is to bring together the many streams of intellectual thought that form Freemasonry.

For information about the Lodge or its meetings, the Foundation, or the Hibiscus Masonic Review, please contact the Secretary by email at sec@ hibiscuslodge.com, or at Hibiscus Lodge No. 275, F. &. A. M., P.O.B.770218, Miami, FL, 33177–0004, or by telephone at 305–971–2335.

ACKNOWLEDGMENTS

I would like to thank the authors of the articles appearing in this journal for their faith in a new venture in Masonic publishing. Their encouragement was invaluable and beyond all expectations. Thanks also go to the Brothers of Hibiscus Lodge No. 275 whose wholehearted backing and support and whose commitment to Masonic education made this publication possible. Finally, my thanks to my wife Maria for her incredible love and support without which none of this would have ever been possible.

Peter J. Millheiser, MD, FACS

BIOGRAPHICAL NOTES

YASHA BERESINER, LL.B. received his law degree from Hebrew University of Jerusalem, Faculty of Law with Postgraduate Law studies at University College, London for 2 years. He spent 2 years in a parachute regiment in the Israel Defense Forces. He has been Director and owner of InterCol London since 1982. His Craft activities include being initiated into Lodge of Faith & Friendship No 7326 (EC) 1975, appointed PGStB, United Grand Lodge of England April 2003, AGDC, Regular Grand Lodge of Italy June 1996; PGSW, (V W Rank) July 2003, Hon SGW (V W Rank) Grand Lodge of the State of Israel Oct 2004, appointed Kellerman Lecturer 2000 (Australia) July 2000, invited to join Quatuor Coronati Lodge No 2076, the premier Lodge of Masonic research in February 1991, being Worshipful Master in 1997–8. In the Royal Arch, he was Exalted Universal Brotherhood 5785 Dec 1977 and MEZ 1989–90, appointed PAGDC Supreme Grand Chapter of England April 2006, and appointed by Supreme Grand Chapter Official Batham Royal Arch Lecturer. In the Mark Degree, he was Advanced in Kenton Lodge of MMM No 901 (Middx) 1981; Worshipful Master in 1988–89, appointed Past Assistant Grand Director of Ceremonies February 1999, and PProGSW (Middlesex) April 2003. He has been a member of many other Masonic organizations. He has been Master of the Worshipful Company of Makers of Playing Cards, one of the City of London's ancient Livery Guilds. Speaking 6 languages, he has lectured on Freemasonry in many countries. His Masonic books include *Masonic Curiosities, Royal Arch 4th Degree of Freemasonry* and *City of London: A Masonic Guide.* He has written articles for many Masonic journals including *Ars Quatuor Coronatorum, Freemasonry Today, Square, The Ashlar, Acta Macionica, Transactions of Civil War Lodge of Research, Diadem, Engenho & Arte, Heredom,* and numerous others. He presently has a series of articles appearing in *Freemasonry Today* on the collections of the various Masonic museums in the United Kingdom. He has written many articles on collectibles and his books on collectibles include *Catalogue of Colombian Currency, The Story of Paper Money, Collectors' Guide to Paper Money,* and *British County Maps—A Guide.* He has also written *The Paper Tiger* on the Arab-Israeli 1967 War. He represented Israel in Judo at the Tokyo Student Olympics in 1967. He is a Qualified City of London Guide and frequently leads walking tours. He is also active in world Scouting. He is a renowned speaker and lecturer and is unique in that his wife Zmira was his sergeant in the Israel Defense Forces. It is unclear who outranked whom.

MARTIN CHERRY, A.B. was born in 1968 in Oxford. He has a BA (Hons) History and Politics from Oxford Polytechnic and BSc. (Econ) Library and Information Science from the University of Wales, Aberystwyth. He came to the Library and Museum of Freemasonry (United Grand Lodge of England) as Assistant Librarian in 2002, having worked in both public and academic libraries. In 2005, he became Librarian. Although he is not a Freemason, being Librarian of the United Grand Lodge of England has given him a rounded education in the subject. He lives in the London Borough of Hillingdon with his wife and daughter. Playing golf is his spare time interest and he also enjoys watching cricket.

MARGARET JACOB, Ph.D. received her B.A. from St. Joseph's College in 1964.and her Ph.D. at Cornell University in 1968. She taught at the University of East Anglia in Norwich. She has been Dean of the College at City University in New York and a member of the Graduate Faculty at the New School for Social Research. She was recruited to UCLA from the University of Pennsylvania where she is *Distinguished Professor of History*. Her interests lie in the history of science and in intellectual history, and she has worked in the fields of British, Dutch, French and Belgian history. Her archival research has taken her to London, Birmingham, Manchester, Amsterdam, The Hague, Brussels, Paris and various French provincial towns. In 2002 she was awarded an honorary doctorate from the University of Utrecht and made a member of the American Philosophical Society and the Hollandse Maatschappij der Weterschappen. She has been visiting faculty at l'École des Hautes Études and the University of Ulster. Currently she holds a grant from the NEH for Collaborative Research on scientific application and early industrialization in Britain. Her overriding intellectual concern has been with the meaning and impact of the Newtonian synthesis on religion, political ideology, industrial development and cultural practices. She has worked extensively on Newton's immediate followers, on freethinkers, freemasons, Dutch and French Newtonians, and has recently published a book with Larry Stewart on the impact of Newton's science from the publication of the *Principia* in 1687 to the Great Exhibition in 1851. She also, along with Lynn Hunt, has an active interest in British radicals and romantics of the 1790s. She has commented on issues in the so-called "science wars" and has written on historical methods and practices. Along with Spencer Weart, she edits a series published by Harvard University Press, aimed at making the history of science more accessible. She also reviews for The *Los Angeles Times*. She is also Principal Investigator for a NIMH project on chronic pain in children in collaboration with UCLA's Pediatric Pain Clinic. She has worked on the cultural resources at play in economic decision making and the role of science in industrial development. In 2004 she was University Research Lecturer. Some of her many published books include *Strangers Nowhere in the World: The Rise of Cosmopolitanism in Early Modern Europe*, published by the University of Pennsylvania Press, 2006, *The Origins of Freemasonry. Facts and Fictions*, University of Pennsylvania Press, 2005, With Larry Stewart, *Practical Matter. The Impact of Newton's Science from 1687 to 1851*, Harvard University Press, November 2004, *Scientific Culture and the Making of the Industrial West*, published by Oxford University Press; 1997, *Newton and the Culture of Newtonianism*, with Betty Jo Teeter Dobbs. Humanity Press, 1995, Winner of the Watson-Davis Award, History of Science Society, *Living the Enlightenment: Freemasonry and Politics in Eighteenth Century Europe*, Oxford University Press, 1991, *The Radical Enlightenment: Pantheists, Freemasons, and Republicans,* The Temple Publishers, 1991 with a new edition in 2006, and *The Cultural Meaning of the Scientific Revolution*, Alfred Knopf/McGraw-Hill, New York, 1988.

PETER J. MILLHEISER, MD, FACS, 32°, received his AB degree from Columbia College where he was on the wrestling and golf teams. He received the MD degree from the Columbia College of Physicians and Surgeons in New York City. He had an orthopaedic surgery residency at the Hospital for Joint Diseases in New York City with further studies at the Wrightington Centre for Hip Surgery in England, the University of Vienna School of Medicine, and Lecco General Hospital in Italy. He is a Diplomate of the American Board of Orthopaedic Surgery, a Fellow of the American Academy of Orthopaedic Surgeons and a Fellow of the American College of Surgeons. He has been an Instructor in Orthopaedic Surgery at the Mt. Sinai School of Medicine in New York and Assistant Clinical Professor at the University of Miami School of Medicine. He has been Chief of Orthopaedic Surgery at the 1207th U. S. Army Hospital. He presently practices in Miami, Florida. His Masonic activities include being Master of Hibiscus Lodge No. 275 in Florida twice, member of Thomas Harper Lodge No. 9612 in the Province of Warwickshire in England, member of the Quatuor Coronati Correspondence Circle, member of the Dormer Masonic Study Circle, member of the Scottish Rite Valley of Miami, Sovereign Master of Mystic Tie Council No. 374, Allied Masonic Degrees, Past High Priest (First Principal) of Jericho Chapter No. 11, Royal Arch Masons, Past Grand Historian and Past Grand Master of the Second Veil of The Most Excellent Grand Chapter of Royal

Arch Masons of Florida. He is a member of Adoniram Council No. 10 Royal and Select Masters and Mahi Temple. He is an active collector of Masonic jewels and is a member of Jewels of the Craft in England. He has lectured widely on spinal problems and on historical topics in Freemasonry. Spare time activities include traveling with his wife Maria, spending time with his granddaughter (Sofia-Maria), sailing, and fishing.

S. BRENT MORRIS, Ph.D. 33°, S. Brent Morris has a PhD and MA in mathematics from Duke University and an MS in Computer Science from Johns Hopkins University. He is believed to have the only doctorate in the world in card shuffling; his dissertation was entitled *Permutations by Cutting and Shuffling: A Generalization to Q Dimensions.* He retired after 25 years as a mathematician with the federal government and has taught at Duke and Johns Hopkins Universities. He is now Director of Membership Development for the Scottish Rite Masons in Washington, D.C., He holds two U.S. patents and is the author of *Magic Tricks, Card Shuffling, and Dynamic Computer Memories* (MAA, 1998), nine technical articles, and nine books on Freemasonry including *The Complete Idiot's Guide to Freemasonry, Masonic Philanthropies,* and *Cornerstones of Freedom,* and is a co-author of *Is It True What They Say About Freemasonry?.* He was an ACM Distinguished Lecturer, an MAA Visiting Lecturer, a SIAM Visiting Lecturer, and he has been invited to lecture at the Smithsonian Institution, the Board on Mathematical Sciences of the National Research Council, NASA Goddard Space Flight Center, AT&T Bell Labs, NEC Research Institute, the National War College, the Joint Mathematics Meetings of the MAA/AMS, and over 100 colleges. He is managing editor of the largest-circulation Masonic magazine in the world, the *Scottish Rite Journal* of the Supreme Council, 33°, S.J., and Editor of *Heredom,* the journal of the Scottish Rite Research Society and *The Plumbline.* He is Treasurer of The Scottish Rite Research Society. He is currently on the graduate faculty at George Washington University. He is Past Master of Patmos Lodge No. 70 of Maryland, and is the Senior Warden of Quatuor Coronati Lodge No. 2076 London, the premier Masonic research lodge, and is the only American member of the lodge. In matters Sherlockian, he is a member of Watson's Tin Box of Ellicott City, Maryland, The Master's Masons, and Moriarty's Mathematicians. He is also an Associate Professorial Lecturer at George Washington University, teaching a graduate course in cryptography.

ANDREW PRESCOTT, Ph.D. is Director of the Centre for Research into Freemasonry at the University of Sheffield, the first such centre to be established in a British university. (http://www.shef.ac.uk/~crf) He studied history at the

University of London and was a curator in the Department of Manuscripts in the British Library from 1979–2000. He was the principal library contact for the British Library's Electronic Beowulf project. He has lectured and published widely on the history of freemasonry since the establishment of the Centre in 2001. He is also one of the country's leading experts on the application of new technologies to humanities research, and is a member of the management team of the University's Humanities Research Institute. He is active as a medieval historian, with a particular interest in the history of the library of Sir Robert Cotton and contributed the articles on the leaders of the rising of 1381 to the new Dictionary of National Biography. He has been an editor of the British Library's Studies in Medieval Culture series. He was a member of the ACO-HUM Working Group on History and Historical Informatics from 1996–99. Among his many publications are 'Brother Irving: Sir Henry Irving and Freemasonry', First Knight: Journal of the Irving Society 7.2 (December 2003), pp. 13–22, *The Benedictional of St Æthelwold: a masterpiece of Anglo-Saxon art*, (London: The British Library, 2002), 'The Unlawful Societies Act of 1799', in *The Social Impact of Freemasonry on the Modern Western World*, ed. M. D. J. Scanlan, The Canonbury Papers I (London: Canonbury Masonic Research Centre, 2002), pp. 116–134, *Preston's Illustrations of Masonry* [CD-ROM] (Sheffield: Academy Electronic Publications, 2001), and 'The Ghost of Asser' in ed. P. Pulsiano and E. Treharne, *Anglo-Saxon Manuscripts and their Heritage*, (Ashgate: Aldershot, 1998), pp. 255–291. On March 1, 2007, he became Manager of Library Services at the University of Wales Lampeter which houses a collection of interesting Masonic material.

R. WILLIAM WEISBERGER, PH.D. was born and reared in Steubenville, Ohio. He is affiliated with Steubenville Lodge # 45 F. & A. M. He belongs to the Steubenville Valley Scottish Rite and to the York Rite bodies in that town. Weisberger also belongs to the Columbus Shrine. He is an Active Member of the Ohio Chapter of Research and of the Scottish Rite Research Society. He received a BSFS from Georgetown University's School of Foreign Service, a Masters Degree in Modern European History from Duquesne University, and a Ph.D. in Modern European Intellectual and Social History from the University of Pittsburgh. His doctoral dissertation focused on Freemasonry in London, Paris, Prague, and Vienna during the Enlightenment. His revised dissertation was published in 1993 as *Speculative Freemasonry and the Enlightenment: A Study of the Craft in London, Paris, Prague, and Vienna,* as a part of Columbia University's East European Monograph Series. He has served as a co-editor of *Freemasonry on*

Both Sides of the Atlantic (2002), of *Hungary's Historical Legacies* (2000), and of a forthcoming study in 2007 concerning profiles of revolutionaries in Atlantic History. Prof. Weisberger has published three major articles for scholarly journals about Freemasonry. He has also written approximately 90 short biographical entries and has published over 100 book reviews for scholarly journals. He is a Professor of History and Sociology at Butler County Community College and is also an Adjunct Professor of History at the University of Pittsburgh.

THE PAST AND THE FUTURE IN MASONIC SCHOLARSHIP

✦

BY MARGARET C. JACOB, Ph.D

Back in the 1970s when first I approached the historical subject of freemasonry, I went to the New York Public Library. That seemed the first obvious place to go. There stood the old card catalogue with its neat drawers filled with 3 by 5 cards that revealed the call numbers of its vast collection. The cards devoted to the subject "freemasonry" occupied a row more than 10 feet long and about 5 feet tall, daunting, and as I quickly realized, from a scholarly point of view, virtually worthless. Let me explain.

At that time the unsuspecting researcher might turn to a standard work in the field of European freemasonry: *Revolution and freemasonry, 1680–1800*, by Bernard Fay (1935). It was widely cited, and by a prolific French historian who had first published on this European theme in French. Indeed the book was on the reading list I used as a graduate student when studying the eighteenth century. Nowhere did anyone mention that Fay had gone on to become a Nazi collaborator and that he subscribed to the myth of there having been a masonic conspiracy behind the French Revolution, indeed at the heart of modernity. But in that vast collection of index cards there was no work that took issue specifically with Fay and the shortcomings and distortions found in his approach. Or take the countless histories of various lodges in just about every Western and some non-Western countries, all easily accessed through those index cards. Often the histories were factual and always they were written by devoted brothers who cared deeply about their lodge and its history. Admirable though they were—when they were accurate—they contained little by the way of historical analysis, nor did they ask, why might someone become a freemason, or in the Anglo-American tradition, what did the exclusion of women mean? Those realities—that of course men would want to be freemasons and women not so—were taken as givens.

Days spent in the card catalogue of major libraries quickly revealed that masonic history was cordoned off, work done by and for the devout, or worse still by the fanatical, often from the far-right. It was easy to conclude that it would be better not to enquire about the meaning of freemasonry in the lives of the thousands who populated the lodges in the first three generations of their existence as social centers for Euro-American men—and eventually women. They came from a wide variety of professions and social classes; notably absent after the founding of the Grand Lodge of London in 1717 were actual stonemasons. But it is hard to dampen down the curiosity of any historian especially when the topic is something like freemasonry. It was new to its age, directly linked to British social experience, and by the mid-eighteenth century immensely popular in the larger European cities. How could the historian not be interested? But how should she proceed with a topic that had become slightly disreputable in the larger scholarly world. Incorrectly, freemasonry had become associated with the mystical or the irrational, or with the devoted or the fanatical. We must never forget that particularly in Europe and Latin America the myth survived until well after World War II: there had been a Jewish-Masonic conspiracy that lay at the corrupt heart of modernity.

Let me fast forward. Today when I teach about the early scholarship on freemasonry I draw on the blackboard, somewhat in jest, a picture of what a card catalogue looks like. My students use only computers to access library records and indeed to find web sites that will help them with the topic of their term papers. Put the word "freemasonry" into Google and we discover over 3 million entries. Within the first ten stand sites devoted to exposing the order as conspiratorial or as a Satanic religion. In one sense not much progress has been made since the days of the card catalogue. The problem remains: how do we distinguish fact from fiction, how do we write about freemasonry within a specific historical context whether that be late eighteenth-century Boston or early nineteenth-century Mexico? The answer lies in appropriating the standards of historical scholarship taught routinely at the university level and bringing them to bear on masonic history and its historical context.

The professionalization of masonic scholarship is now happening. There has been an enormous change in the habits of masonic research since the 1970s. First of all, it has become respectable, and second and most important, standards of historical evidence and scholarly rigor have been brought to its study. These changes have occurred on both sides of the Atlantic, but they are more visible in respectable academic settings in Europe. At universities such as Sheffield, Leiden, Bordeaux, and Zaragoza in Spain, scholarly centers for the study of freemasonry are active and supported by both the university and private donors. The European Science Foundation has just given a major grant to study the phenomenon of freemasonry within national contexts.

In America younger scholars can now be found who are doing dissertations or books on aspects of masonic history. Going to the electronic site http://wwwlib.umi.com/dissertations/results?set_num=1 we discover that over fifty Ph.D. dissertations that deal with aspects of masonic history have been produced during the past ten years in American universities. Let me give but one example with which I am familiar because its author, Jacob Dorman, read with me in preparation for researching and writing "The Black Israelists of Harlem and the professors of Oriental and African mystic science in the 1920s," UCLA 2004. This work in American black history chronicles the search undertaken by black intellectuals alive during the Harlem renaissance. They turned to freemasonry, as well as various forms of religious experience, as they searched for new truths and new identities that promised liberation.

There are other causes for optimism about the course of masonic research worldwide. Increasingly attention is being paid to masonic lodges in imperial settings as well as lodges founded in non-Western countries by local people interested in the meaning of freemasonry within their own cultural setting. New research is also underway on women's freemasonry. And finally, there are the "Moscow archives"—to use the shorthand of those of us who work with them.

These archives contain thousands of hand-written (later typed) documents from countries occupied by the Nazis. They fervently believed in the Jewish-Masonic conspiracy and sought to prove its existence and detail its evil intentions. To that end in 1940 the Nazis raided the Grand Lodges as well as local lodges in the countries they occupied. All this documentation was shipped back to Berlin where an institute was established to study the stolen archives. Then came the Russian army. Most of the contents of what had been in the institute was confiscated by the Russians and shipped back to Moscow, probably intended as post-war bargaining chips in negotiations to secure Russian treasures stolen by the retreating German army. But somehow the process did not work that way and masonic records from France, Belgium and The Netherlands were locked away until the 1990s. The American historian, Patricia Kennedy Grimsted (see her *Trophies of War and Empire*, Harvard University Press, 2001), alerted the world to their existence. After financial pressure was applied to the Putin government now most of the archives have been returned, to Paris, Brussels, and The

Hague. This is an extraordinary set of manuscripts, equaling thousands of documents, some from as early as the 1730s and never seen since the 1930s. I have used them in two recent books and doubtless dozens of other scholars will do the same.

The Moscow archives now further brighten the future of masonic research into the European past and they suggest the necessity of preserving archives, carefully and quickly. Someday all those local histories of individual lodges will need to be rewritten. Guidance will come from the older histories written by dedicated brothers, but as we employ the working methods of good scholars everywhere we will also need the original documents. If thousands of hand-written texts can survive a world war, two confiscations, not to mention the rigor of cold storage in Moscow winters, then we can only hope and assume that all the lodges in this country now in possession of historical documents will work very hard to preserve them and to make them accessible to all reputable brothers or scholars. The masonic past has a future only if we give it one.

Reprinted with permission from a Special Preview Edition of Cosmopolis: The Quarterly Bulletin of the Roosevelt Center. The Roosevelt Center for the Study of Civil Society and Freemasonry is a beginning institution in California that potentially will be a formal research center at UCLA. Since the mid-twentieth century, the subject of Freemasonry has gained enhanced respectability as a field of serious historical inquiry, and part of a wider investigation into the emergence and evolution of civil society. Sixty Ph.D. dissertations produced in American universities during the past decade have focused on Freemasonry. There has been little communication, however, between the American Masonic community and professional academic institutions. The goal of the Roosevelt Center is to serve as a focal point for conversation, inquiry and action by students, faculty, Masons and others interested in the emerging scholarly fields of civil society and Freemasonry. The Center approaches Freemasonry as an association historically representative of civil society as it developed from the eighteenth-century onwards. It supports inquiry into the role Freemasonry assumed in private and public life. It also explores Masonic thought in a variety of historical and contemporary settings. The approach of the Center is multi-disciplinary, comparative and intended to support work at multiple institutions as well as with independent scholars. http://rooseveltcenter.org/

PARISIAN MASONRY, THE LODGE OF THE NINE SISTERS, AND THE FRENCH ENLIGHTENMENT

◆

BY R. WILLIAM WEISBERGER, Ph.D

A. The Evolution of Masonic Systems in Paris

1. The Origins and Operations of the Grand Lodge of France

Modern London Masonry during the 1720s and the 1730s affected the development of the Craft in Paris. With approval from the Grand Lodge of London, the Grand Lodge of France was established in 1725 in Paris.[1] With the consent of the Modern London Grand Lodge, Lord Derwentwater, an Englishman residing in Paris, was appointed as Grand Master of the French Grand Lodge. He, in turn, named the Duke d'Antin and several English and French nobles living in Paris as officers of this new grand lodge. Derwentwater, until approximately 1736, dominated the affairs of this Parisian grand lodge.[2] More importantly, the Grand Lodge of France, whose administrative operations between 1725 and 1736 were quite routine, emerged as a source of Anglophilism. This body received at this time administrative direction from the Grand Lodge of London and established lodges in Paris to promote significant ideas associated with English culture.[3]

The Lodges *Louis d"Argent, Coustos-Villeroy,* and *Bussi-Aumont* operated in Paris between 1727 and 1740 and were important to Masons in the French capital for several reasons. The organizational functions of these lodges resembled those of London lodges and, for the most part, permitted Parisian Masons, who were accustomed to monarchical institutions, to engage in new activities. Parisian lodges permitted Masons to elect their members and officers, to learn about natural liberties, to enact laws according to the majority rule principle, and to serve on committees. Those Masons serving as lodge officers, in many instances, were entrusted with new responsibilities and roles of leadership. Parisian lodges especially functioned as social centers. These bodies functioned as clubs, sponsoring many banquets and some lectures and thus allowing English and French Masons to interact with each other. Parisian lodges recruited many aristocrats, numerous middle class individuals, and some intellectuals. There was, however, another important facet of Parisian lodge life. Parisian Masons looked to these lodges for explanations of doctrines and symbols of the Blue Degrees.

Some concepts and symbols of the Modern degrees proved to be of special importance to Parisian Masons. These Masons seemed to perceive the Blue Degrees as a special source of the ideas of antiquity.[4] Parisian Masons learned from these degrees about important ideas concerning ancient architecture, mathematics, and science; moreover, the Blue Degrees explained to them ancient concepts regarding justice, temperance, and virtue.[5] Deism was quite fashionable in Paris, and the tenets of this ancient moral philosophy were well presented in the Blue Degrees. As a result of their exposure to the All Seeing Eye, to the three lesser lights of Masonry, and to the square and compasses, Parisian Masons were given ritualistic explanations concerning Deity, the powers of Nature, and the proper moral conduct of man. Ancient deistic concepts of the Blue Degrees consequently served as an alternative to the teachings of modern religion. These concepts also helped to shape the views of Parisian Masons towards the state and influenced their ethical conduct.[6]

Modern enlightenment ideas appearing in the Blue Degrees stimulated the interest of Parisian Masons and, in many instances, were identified with a civil religion in France. These degrees revealed to Masons in the French capital significant Enlightenment concepts pertaining to education. In light of their exposure to the middle chamber of the Temple of Solomon and to the globe, Parisian Masons learned that knowledge is derived from reason and the senses and that Masons should strive to promote the study of the liberal arts and should probe Nature to ascertain her laws.[7] To aristocratic and bourgeois Masons in Paris, the Blue Degrees contained important social and political ideas. Parisian Masons were taught to be benevolent, just, and prudent and to work for the implementation of liberty, religious toleration, and other natural rights. These Masons evolved secular interpretations in explaining the moral legends, tenets, and symbols of the Blue Degrees and, in many cases, became ardent proponents of natural liberties. Numerous Masonic symbols helped to exemplify concepts of a French civil religion based on political reforms. The square, the plumb, the gavel, and the columns of Solomon's Temple were associated with this religion and appeared frequently during the *ancien régime* and the French Revolution.[8]

Some members of Parisian lodges during the 1720s and 1730s performed cultural functions to promote Enlightenment concepts. Established in 1727, the Parisian Lodge *Louis d'Argent* consisted of numerous nobles of the robe and of some middle class intellectuals. French judges belonging to this lodge meeting in the *Hôtel de Bussy* furthermore served as patrons of the arts and sciences. Judge Davy de la Fautrière belonged to the *Club de l'Entresol*, was a proponent of economic and legal reforms, and published a history of French commerce and finance. He also revealed interest in Newtonian concepts, publishing an article in 1739 in the *Journal de Trévoux* concerning the importance of mechanical laws to metaphysics.[9] Count Chauvelin, also a judge in the Parisian Parlement, behaved as a Masonic enlightener; he was an associate member of the Academy of Sciences and also possessed interests in history and in literature. Chauvelin allocated funds for the publication of *Charles XII* by Voltaire. He furthermore developed a large library containing works about the Enlightenment and prior to his death donated them to the lodge.[10]

Two other minor intellectuals were involved with the *Louis d'Argent* Lodge. Jacques Pernetti was a Benedictine priest who left Rome to reside first in Lyon and then in Paris. He was admitted to the lodge in 1730 and was known as a minor writer; Pernetti in 1732 published *Repos de Cyrus*, lauding the accomplishments of the ancient king. Pernetti also wrote a short work about Masonry, claiming in *Les Conseils de l'Amitié* that the Craft functioned to promote benevolent and cultural activities.[11] The former Jesuit and poet Jean Gresset evidently envisioned Masonry as a cultural vehicle of the Enlightenment. He maintained that Masonry taught its members ancient philosophical views espoused by Aristotle, Plato, and Socrates. According to Gresset, Masonry revolved around important concepts of the Enlightenment.

> Reason reigns supreme and is needed for the study of Nature.
> Reason reveals to men their natural rights and liberties …
> Masons, use reason to erect your spiritual temples and to improve society....[12]

Montesquieu, who was inducted into the Horn Lodge in 1730, visited the *Louis d'Argent* Lodge in 1734. Several reasons might be suggested to explain his interest in Masonry and his visit to this Parisian lodge. Montesquieu during the late 1720s visited England, became friendly with the Duke of Richmond and Desaguliers, and evidently was convinced by these two Masonic enlighteners to affiliate with the Craft.[13] From an ideological viewpoint, Montesquieu evidently sympathized with Masonic teachings pertaining to the Enlightenment. Like many Masons, he was interested in experimental science and believed that the laws of Newton could be applied to the study of other disciplines. Like many Masons, Montesquieu exhibited interest in the political thought of the ancients and in 1748 argued in *L'Esprit des lois* that the Greeks and Romans should be commended for issuing constitutions, for developing viable legal systems, and for implementing the principle of the separation of powers.[14] He became an Anglophile; he believed that the government of early eighteenth century England resembled successful ancient ones and succeeded in operating in light of the doctrine of the separation of powers and in protecting the natural liberties of its citizens.[15] As an enlightener and as a Mason, Montesquieu subscribed to the doctrine of religious toleration; he denounced in *L'Esprit des lois* the persecution of the Jews in Europe. Montesquieu also explained in *Lettres persanes* that the teachings of Judaism, Islam, and Christianity were similar to each other and that European monarchs during the eighteenth century should enact laws to recognize the civic rights of religious groups in their states.[16] In knowing that several French enlighteners and some of his judicial colleagues from the Parlement belonged to the *Louis d'Argent*, Montesquieu visited this lodge. He knew, moreover, that the *Louis d'Argent* and other lodges in Paris sponsored some Enlightenment activities. After his visit to the *Louis d'Argent*, Montesquieu appeared, however, to lose interest in the affairs of the Craft and evidently was disappointed to see that no Parisian lodge functioned as a Masonic learned society.[17]

Established in 1736, the Lodge *Bussi-Aumont* consisted, for the most part, of French aristocrats affiliated with the army and of a few enlighteners. A prominent French general, Bertin du Rocheret, played a central role in the lodge and recruited to its ranks French nobles of the sword.[18] A member of the Rocheret circle, Charles Francois de Calvière served as a general in the French army and displayed interest in Enlightenment activities. Admitted to the *Bussi-Aumont* in 1737, Calvière also belonged to the French Academy of Painting and was known for his collection of paintings and busts. An obscure English painter, Mr. Collins belonged to this lodge and presumably during the 1730s was in Paris to study art.[19] The *Bussi-Aumont* Lodge, by and large, failed to recruit many enlighteners and consequently did not stage many cultural events. This lodge also had a small membership and engaged in minimal relations with the Lodges *Louis d'Argent* and *Coustos-Villeroy*.

The *Coustos-Villeroy* Lodge was established in 1736, consisted of approximately twenty French Masons, and seemed to develop into a center for numerous

European Masonic aristocrats residing in Paris. Some enlighteners as well were affiliated with this lodge; a group of French opera singers was associated with the *Coustos-Villeroy* and consisted of Jean Guignon, Jacques Naudot, and Pierre Jeliote.[20] Joseph Burr was a Huguenot banker, providing the lodge with financial assistance and writing several articles about deism.[21] A friend of Baur, the lawyer Pierre Meyzieu was a minor proponent of legal reforms and a financial contributor to the *Encyclopédie*.[22] Residing in Paris during the late 1730s, Central and East European nobles in some cases were patrons of the arts and sciences and exhibited interest in affiliating with the *Coustos-Villeroy*. It seemed that the Duke of Villeroi encouraged many of his aristocratic friends to become involved with the lodge. As a result of his efforts, the *Coustos-Villeroy* in 1737 inducted into its ranks the Venetian ambassador Count Farsetti, Prince Caraffa of Lombardy, the Swedish diplomat Baron Scheffer, the Danish ambassador Count Platte, Prince Wemille of Nassau, Prince Lubomirski of Poland, and Prince Nariskin of Russia. The lodge consequently reflected a diverse ethnic composition, and many of these aristocratic Masons also belonged to Parisian learned societies.[23]

There were, however, challenges posed to the operations of the Lodges *Coustos-Villeroy* and *Louis d'Argent* during the 1730s. Authorities of the Catholic Church and administrators of the Bourbon Monarchy suspiciously viewed the activities of these bodies. Yet the alleged connection between the Jacobites and Parisian Masonry posed a serious threat to the functioning of these lodges.

Although concrete evidence has not been produced to demonstrate the precise relationship between Parisian Masonry and the Jacobite movement, there probably were some members of the *Coustos-Villeroy* and *Louis d'Argent* Lodges who supported efforts to restore the Stuarts to the English throne.[24] What might be suggested is that a Jacobite faction arose in Parisian Masonry in 1736, was headed by Lord Derwentwater, and attracted support from members of the *Coustos-Villeroy* and *Louis d'Argent* Lodges. That year, another Masonic group consisting of members from both of these lodges ascended to oppose and to discredit the Jacobite faction. As a result of the successful efforts of the anti-Jacobite group, Derwentwater probably was forced to resign as Grand Master. Moreover, his successor, the Duke d'Antin, evidently initiated measures to suppress French Masons involved with the Jacobites and to exonerate Parisian Masonry from the attacks of political and religious authorities.[25]

Louis XV in 1737 was concerned about the operations of Masonic lodges in Paris. The king, who in many instances had provided assistance to sympathizers of the Stuart cause, was probably not disturbed about the alleged connection between the Jacobites and Masons, but for other motives favored the probing of

Masonic activities in the French capital. Louis presumably was apprehensive about the teachings of Masonry, believing that its rites contained antimonarchistic doctrines. Moreover, he probably was concerned about the composition of Masonic lodges, thinking that many members of the Craft were *frondeurs* and might use these lodges to conspire for the overthrow of his throne. The 1737 Decree issued against Masonry reflected the concerns of the king. This decree stipulated that royal advisers and administrators were forbidden from belonging to Masonic lodges and that the police would be empowered to search these bodies for traitors.[26]

Rene Hérault, the head of the police in the French capital, conducted investigations of Parisian Masonry between 1737 and 1743 and showed that Masons were not involved with seditious activities. During these investigations, Hérault made no arrests, submitted frequent reports to *L'Arsenal*, and revealed important perceptions about Parisian Masonry.

> The Masonic order was established in England and first appeared in Paris in 1725.... Three lodges have operated in the city, have conferred degrees based on the teachings of King Solomon, and have prided themselves for their charitable activities.... Members of the order in Paris have thought of themselves as brothers and are comprised of nobles, of merchants, and of individuals in the arts and sciences.... Important and less known individuals have been received into the order, and some of my friends have been admitted to it.... Count Maurepas, the Duke of Villeroi, and Bertin du Rocheret have been active in the order and have told me that political matters are not discussed in Masonic assemblies....[27]

The reactions of Louis to the reports of Hérault were mixed; the king, on the one hand, was probably surprised to know that some prominent nobles of the robe and his friend the Duke of Villeroi actively participated in Parisian Masonry. Louis, on the other hand, evidently was relieved to be informed that the operations of the order were not subversive. For six years, he received reports from the Paris police commissioner, but as a result of the influence of Villeroi, d'Antin, and other French Masonic nobles decided in approximately 1739 not to take action to suppress the Craft. During the remainder of his reign Louis maintained cordial relations with members of the Craft and more importantly permitted the operations of Masonic lodges in Paris and in other French cities.[28]

Like the edict issued by the French king in 1737, the bull announced by the pope in 1738 posed a threat to the functioning of Parisian lodges. This bull of Clement XII stipulated that Catholics were forbidden to affiliate with Masonic lodges and that Catholic monarchs and clergymen would cooperate to suppress the order.[29] The bull did not, however, thwart the growth of Parisian Masonry; Louis XV and ranking church officials seemed to ignore its provisions. Moreover, the gradual increase of the rosters of Parisian lodges in 1740 suggested that Catholic Masons in the French capital disregarded the provisions of the bull and that the operations and rites of the Craft satisfied their cultural and emotional needs.

The enigmatic career of Andrew Michael Ramsay illustrated quite a bit about Catholicism, Masonry, and the Enlightenment. On the one hand, Ramsay was a Catholic enlightener and, on the other, contributed to raising the status of Parisian Masonry during the late 1730s and early 1740s. The son of a Calvinist baker and an Anglican mother, Ramsay was reared in Ayr, Scotland, attended for a short time the Universities of Edinburg and Leyden, and in light of his exposure to the views of Boerhaave became a proponent of deistic and mechanistic ideas. The incessant travels of Ramsay helped to shape his thinking; this adventurer and enlightener studied under Fenelon in Cambrai, became a Catholic, went to Rome in about 1724 to serve as a tutor for the sons of the old Pretender James, and during his stay in Italy seemed to support the Jacobite cause. Ramsay, during the late 1720s resided in England and seemed to be well received in the world of the British Enlightenment. He was awarded a doctorate in civil law from Oxford, was admitted to the Royal Society and to the Gentlemen's Society of Spalding, and was inducted into the Horn Lodge.[30] Ramsay left London in 1730 and from that year until his death in 1743 lived in Paris. As a result of his friendships with Masons who opposed the designs of Derwentwater, Ramsay in 1736 denounced the activities of the Jacobites and the next year was appointed as Orator of the French Grand Lodge. He used this position to support Parisian Masons against their political and religious foes, proclaiming that the teachings of Masonry were not subversive. Ramsay also believed as a Catholic enlightener that the principles of the Craft reflected salient doctrines of Catholicism and those of other major religions of the world.[31]

Like Desaguliers and other Modern English Masonic enlighteners, Ramsay perceived the ancients as significant contributors to Masonic thought. In *Les Voyages de Cyrus*, published in 1731, Ramsay claims that Egyptian priests, Solomon, Cyrus, and other ancient monarchs and sages were familiar with the teachings of the ancient mysteries. He further maintains that many ancient kings and philosophers worshiped the Supreme Creator, subscribed to the moral doctrines of deism, promoted the study of Nature, and thus helped to lay the foundations of Modern Speculative Freemasonry.

> The teachings of the ancient mysteries were the remnants of an ancient religion practiced by Noah and the patriarchs. These teachings were transmitted from one society to another in the ancient world.... Egyptian priests held great feasts to induct candidates into their mystery cults.... Inspired by the teachings of Moses and David, Solomon ordered the erection of a magnificent temple which was dedicated to the Supreme Creator and whose parts symbolized the operations of Nature and the moral conduct of men. After the temple was completed, Solomon instructed his priests to admit learned Jews and gentiles into its chambers and to convey to these select individuals the teachings of the mysteries.... After the destruction of the first temple, Cyrus, who was initiated into the ancient mysteries by Zorobabel, ordered the rebuilding of the temple and served as a great philosopher king who attempted to improve the status of Masonry and learning in the ancient world....[32]

The Masonic thought of Ramsay also emphasized the importance of the Craft during the Middle Ages. In *Le Discours*, published in 1738 or the same year that the papal bill was promulgated, Ramsay claims that the Templars functioned as a significant brotherhood and that members of this order were loyal to the Catholic church, lived according to the principles of Masonry, and in many cases were French nobles. To Ramsay, the Templars promoted the ancient concepts of benevolence, justice, and virtue and also believed that the teachings of Masonry were compatible with the doctrines of monarchy and with those of Catholicism.[33] In *Le Discours*, Ramsay presented some new interpretations of Masonic philosophy and attempted to justify salient doctrines of the Craft to the hierarchy of the Catholic Church, to Louis XV, and to French aristocratic and bourgeois Catholics. Moreover, he helped to provide Masonry with new direction and to lay the foundations of Scottish Rite Masonry.

2. The Scottish Rite and Masonic Rivalry in Paris

Scottish Rite Masonry, which in fact had little to do with Scotland, originated during the early 1740s in Paris.[34] This new system, which by the late eighteenth century would consist of thirty-two degrees, served as an alternative to Modern Masonry in Paris. Scottish Rite Masonry developed, however, upon the foundations of Modern Masonry and used legends, ideas, and symbols from ancient and medieval history to explain in other ways major concepts appearing in the Blue Degrees. Moreover, the Scottish Rite was intended to provide Parisian Masons with a distinctive Masonic heritage and identity, but on many occasions provoked considerable dissension within the Parisian Masonic community.[35]

The evolution of Scottish Rite Masonry led to the formation of a new grand lodge in Paris. The English Grand Lodge of France was established in 1743 to

replace the French Grand Lodge and strangely enough succeeded in securing recognition from officers of the Grand Lodge of London and in acquiring support
from Parisian leaders of Scottish Rite Masonry. The Duke of Clermont that year
was appointed as the Grand Master of the new grand lodge and was expected to
effect a compromise between the Blue Lodge and Scottish Rite factions. A patron
of the arts and sciences and a cousin of Louis XV, the Duke of Clermont seemed
to be an excellent choice for this position and introduced measures to strengthen
the English Grand Lodge of France.[36]

Clermont for several reasons issued the 1743 and 1755 statutes; he wished to
centralize the new grand lodge, to entrust local lodges with the power of conferring the English and Scottish degrees, and to secure aristocratic and bourgeois
support for Parisian Masonry. The 1743 Statutes gave immense powers to the
Grand Master, enabling him to hold his position for life and to appoint grand
lodge officers and special committees. The statutes further confirmed the regulations specified in the 1723 *Constitutions* and permitted the staging of the Blue
Degrees and of three Scottish Degrees.[37] The 1755 Statutes reconfirmed the
powers of Clermont and his grand lodge officers and defined the duties of officers
of local lodges. These statutes also acknowledged the conferring of the Blue
Degrees and of five Scottish Degrees and required Parisian Masons to comply
with the provisions of a new ethical code issued by the grand lodge.[38] The enac-
tion of the 1743 and 1755 Statutes suggested that the English Grand Lodge of
France provided Parisian Masonry until approximately 1757 with valuable
administrative direction and succeeded in housing under the same roof leaders of
the English and Scottish Rite factions.

However, factional disputes within the English Grand Lodge of France
occurred in late 1758 and brought an end to the era of compromise in Paris.
Some factions remained loyal to Clermont and continued to confer the Modern
Blue Degrees and the first five Scottish Degrees. But others severed ties with the
English Grand Lodge of France and established bodies known as councils and
chapters to stage the higher degrees of Scottish Rite Masonry. As a consequence
of these factional feuds, rivalry among lodges, chapters, and councils persisted
within the Parisian Masonic community until the early 1770s.

Various features characterized the organizational operations and membership
of Parisian lodges, councils, and chapters during the 1760s. The titles and powers
of local lodge officers in Paris were similar to those of local lodge officials in London. Councils of the Emperor of the East and West and Chapters of the Rose
Croix, on the other hand, gave their officers medieval titles; officers of these two
bodies were known as princes, commanders, and knights and were granted pow-

ers resembling those of officials in Parisian lodges.[39] Parisian lodges, chapters, and councils adhered to strict recruiting procedures, and competition for members among these bodies was excessive. Further, the composition of these three bodies somewhat differed. Parisian lodges, for the most part, consisted of middle class officers and members, while councils and chapters in the French capital conversely were comprised of aristocratic officers and members.[40] Parisian chapters and councils sponsored some banquets and lectures, but the noble army leaders, judges, and royal advisers who belonged to these institutions primarily viewed them as centers for the staging of colorful ceremonies associated with the high degrees of Masonry.[41]

The Scottish Degrees presented new interpretations of Masonic doctrines and contained ethical concepts associated with a French civil religion. The Scottish Degrees of the Secret Master, the Perfect Master, and the Perfect Elect were conferred in Parisian lodges. These three degrees revolved around teachings concerning the Temple of Solomon and provided further insight into concepts developed in the Blue Degrees. In the Secret Master Degree, Masons learned that the secrets of the Craft and the Temple of Solomon should never be divulged to individuals not affiliated with the order. This degree further emphasized that Masons should provide for and protect their families and should obey the laws of the state.[42] By stressing the civic virtues of ambition, honesty, and hard work, the Perfect Master Degree offered pertinent explanations of ethical behavior to Catholic and Protestant bourgeois Masons and illustrated to them the importance of their economic positions in French society.[43] Like the Modern rites, the Perfect Elect Degree explained concepts regarding the conduct of Masons in the state. This Scottish Degree emphasized the doctrines of benevolence, justice, and liberty and encouraged members of the Craft to work for the creation of a republic of humanity.[44]

By emphasizing Christian doctrines in many of their degrees, councils and chapters operating in the French capital succeeded in giving to Parisian Masonry a distinctive ideological character. The Degree of the Knights of the East and West and that of the Prince of Jerusalem were staged in Parisian councils. The Knights of the East and West Degree centered on ethical teachings common to the major religions of the world. Knights of the East and West met in the Holy Land during the Crusades and were taught that Moses, Jesus, and Mohammed were great prophets and preached similar moral and religious doctrines. The knights recognized that these religious leaders were inspired by the Deity governing all nations and imbued their followers with the teachings of brotherhood, charity, justice, and virtue.[45] The Prince of Jerusalem Degree was based on a meeting of Christian monarchs during the Crusades. These kings agreed that bravery, honor, and love of their religion motivated Christian knights in their efforts to secure control of Jerusalem.[46] The Knight of the Rose Croix Degree was the most significant one performed in Parisian chapters and was based on the activities of the Templar Order and on those of its leader Jacques De Molai. This degree emphasized that the ancient Roman eagle symbolized honor and military strength and that the rose represented heroic conduct and the sacrificing of life in battle. The Rose Croix Degree further revealed that despite the burning of De Molai at the stake and their subsequent suppression during the early fourteenth century, French Templars during the Crusades had exhibited loyalty to the Catholic Church and to their kings.[47] As a consequence of the moral and religious teachings of this degree, Parisian chapters especially enlisted the support of French Masons belonging to the armed services.

The evolution of the Scottish Degrees produced major effects upon Parisian Masonry. These degrees, on the one hand, contained Christian principles, but, on the other hand, offered vivid explanations of moral and secular concepts. The ancient and medieval tenets of these degrees concerning deism, honor, virtuous conduct, civil obedience, and religious toleration seemed to reflect a character of cultural universality and were associated with ideas of the Enlightenment. The concepts of the Scottish Degrees also were intimately involved with ethical behavior and enabled Parisian Masons to be identified with a distinctive French Masonic culture and community.[48] While its degrees were associated with significant cultural functions, Scottish Rite Masonry caused jurisdictional feuds among bodies of the Craft in the French capital. These feuds, in turn, led during the early 1770s to the fragmentation of Parisian Masonry and threatened to destroy it.

3. The Grand Orient and the Parisian Masonic Compromise

The Duke of Chartres helped to resolve the factional disputes within Parisian Masonry. The Duke of Clermont, who refused to negotiate with leaders of Parisian councils and chapters, died in 1771 and that year was succeeded as Grand Master of the English Grand Lodge of France by the Duke of Chartres. Unlike his predecessor, Chartres was willing to meet with Parisian Scottish Rite leaders and in 1772 entered into parleys with them. The results of these negotiations led to the Parisian Masonic compromise of 1773. The Duke of Chartres and Scottish Rite officials agreed that the Grand Orient would be established as the new governing body of Parisian Masonry. They also wished to transform the Grand Orient into a French national grand lodge. Chartres and Parisian Scottish Rite officials consequently agreed that the Duke of Montmorency-Luxembourg, who was appointed as general-administrator of the Grand Orient, should be authorized to consult with Masonic leaders outside of Paris, so that lodges, councils, and chapters in various provinces of France could be given the opportunity to affiliate with the new grand lodge.[49]

Montmorency-Luxembourg, who proved to be a very capable grand lodge administrator, drafted in 1773 the constitution of the Grand Orient. According to the provisions of this document, administrators of the Grand Orient were empowered to recognize other grand lodges, were to authorize the conferring of the Blue and Scottish Degrees in local Masonic bodies, and were to work in conjunction with an annually elected grand lodge assembly to formulate policy. The constitution further stipulated that grand lodge officers were to review and to give their approval to the constitutions and rosters of local lodges and that grand lodge inspectors were to be sent to local lodges to investigate their affairs and to file reports about their operations.[50]

Major effects resulted during the 1770s from the effective governance and operations of the Grand Orient. By holding annual assemblies, administrators of the Grand Orient permitted representatives of local Masonic bodies to participate in the decision-making process and helped to bring stability to Parisian and French provincial Masonry. By recognizing local bodies which conferred the Blue and Scottish Degrees, leaders of the Grand Orient succeeded in reducing rivalry and internal dissension within Masonry and in transforming this body into an operable and a centralized institution. As a consequence of the efforts of the Dukes of Chartres and Montmorency-Luxembourg, the Grand Orient received the tacit support of the crown, successfully resisted the few attacks of anti-Masonic groups, and continued to induce aristocratic and bourgeois Frenchmen to affiliate with provincial and Parisian lodges.

Masonry and the Enlightenment during the middle years of the 1770s proved to be of importance to Paris. The viability of the Grand Orient and the operations of learned societies and salons in the French capital enabled Paris to evolve into a Masonic and an Enlightenment hub. Jerome Lalande, who was an Orator of the Grand Orient, realized that Parisian Masonry had enlisted the support of numerous enlighteners. In recognizing the need for a Masonic learned society in Paris, Lalande in 1776 proposed the establishment of the Lodge of the Nine Sisters and thus began his efforts to fulfill the idea of his deceased friend Helvétius.[51]

B. The Origins, Organization, and Operations of the Parisian Lodge of the Nine Sisters

1. The Establishment of the Lodge of the Nine Sisters

For varying reasons, the astronomer and Grand Orient administrator Lalande favored the creation of a Parisian Masonic learned society. He believed that the promotion of the liberal arts and sciences was a fundamental objective of Masonry. Lalande further thought that the operations of a Masonic learned society would enable this laudable aim to be accomplished and would reveal to Masons and to intellectuals not belonging to the Craft the intimate connection between Masonry and the French Enlightenment. What Lalande evidently envisioned was a Masonic lodge explicitly designed to service the cause of the Enlightenment; his intention also was to have this lodge serve as the cultural locus of Masonry in Paris. Lalande, moreover, thought that a Parisian Masonic learned society would provide prominent and obscure Masonic intellectuals with the opportunity to interact with each other, to deliver lectures about various topics, to display paintings and sculpture, to perform scientific experiments, and to sponsor special projects pertinent to Masonry and to the Enlightenment. He evidently did not anticipate problems concerning the recruitment of members for his proposed society. This enlightener expected to recruit Masons affiliated with the Paris Academy of Sciences and with other learned societies in the French capital. Lalande also thought that Masonic intellectuals belonging to French provincial academies and to European and American learned societies would like to serve as members of a Parisian Masonic academy. In light of his involvement in the Salon of Madame Helvétius, or the "Estates General of the *philosophes*," Lalande knew that support of many of its Masonic enlighteners could be enlisted for his proposed society.[52]

> At Auteuil, an intimate academic atmosphere was created to enable the blossoming of the arts and sciences. Cabanis and Lalande were moving spirits of the salon. Volney gave historical lectures there; and Garat, Franklin, and Tracy engaged in stimulating philosophical debates. These and other guests of the salon discussed, listened, and truly philosophized....[53]

Lalande on March 11, 1776 submitted to officers of the Grand Orient his proposal concerning the establishment of a Parisian Masonic learned society and met with opposition from some of its conservative administrators. Lalande responded to his opponents in terms of the language of Masonry, but failed to explain why these administrators objected to his proposal.

> My proposal concerning the creation of the Nine Sisters met with opposition. I favored erecting a temple but found it necessary to imitate the example of Zorobabel. I held the trowel in one hand, and the sword in the other....[54]

Motives concerning the opposition to the proposal of Lalande might be suggested. Conservative officers of the Grand Orient knew that the functions of this proposed society would vastly differ from those of regular Masonic lodges. They might have believed that if established, this Parisian learned society would be difficult to administer and might not adhere to grand lodge regulations. Opponents of this proposal realized that French Masonry just recently had been reunited and had been fortunate to operate in an atmosphere relatively free of anti-Masonic attacks; they further might have thought that members of this society would embrace political causes offensive to the French Crown and would precipitate major problems for the Grand Orient. Conservative administrators finally might have viewed the proposed name of the learned society as being strange and might have disliked Lalande.[55]

Officers of the Grand Orient between March and July engaged in debate about the recommendation of Lalande. There were at least three heated sessions about the establishment of the Nine Sisters, and Lalande with great adamancy defended his proposal. With obvious reluctance, officers of the Grand Orient by a five to four vote approved on July 5, 1776 the creation of the Lodge of the Nine Sisters and that same day issued its constitution.[56]

2. The Structure and Leadership of the Nine Sisters

The constitution of the lodge explained the aims of the Nine Sisters. According to this document, Masons admitted to the society were to devote their attention to studying natural and moral laws, to investigating the arts and sciences, and to engaging in cooperative enterprises for the promotion of the Craft and the Enlightenment. These objectives were defined in the constitution in light of Masonic and ancient philosophical concepts.

> The Lodge of the Nine Sisters in making virtue its base has dedicated itself to fostering the arts and sciences. The aim of the lodge is to restore them to their place of dignity. Did not the arts and sciences serve as the foundations of great civilizations and nations?

Work then with zeal to preserve and to advance civilization and our fraternity. Remember then that the base supports the edifice. Decorate both remembering that ornaments should not mask the dignity of Freemasonry....[57]

Appearing on the first page of the constitution, the emblem of the Nine Sisters contained Masonic symbols relating to the objectives of the society. A pyramid appeared on the lodge emblem and represented moral perfection and the orderly operations of Nature. Inscribed within the pyramid were the square, compasses, and the motto "Truth, Union, and Force."[58] By employing these tools in their work, members of the Nine Sisters were to demonstrate the validity of the ancient, Masonic, and Enlightenment belief that virtuous men could cooperate to advance the arts and sciences.[59]

The constitution revealed how this Parisian society would operate as a Masonic lodge. This document stipulated that the lodge would comply with the regulations of the Grand Orient, that stated meetings of the Nine Sisters would be devoted to operational matters, and that special meetings and assemblies would be held to stage degrees and cultural events. During stated meetings, the lodge was to adhere to Masonic procedures, allowing its members to hear committee reports, permitting them to engage in debate about recommendations, and enforcing the principle of majority rule for the adoption of policies and resolutions. The Lodge of the Nine Sisters was to operate according to the principle of benevolence and during stated meetings was empowered to initiate measures to require its lawyers and physicians to render their services without charge to its members.[60] The constitution also provided that during stated meetings, the lodge would adhere to the principle of unanimity for the election of new members and that during special meetings and assemblies, candidates, who were elected as active members of the Nine Sisters but who were never affiliated with the Craft, could be inducted by the lodge into Masonry.

The constitution indicated how the Lodge of the Nine Sisters would function as a learned society. According to the lodge charter, the lodge was not to restrict membership to French Masons, but was to recruit members of the order from other European states and from America. Although the constitution mentioned nothing about membership quotas, the lodge during most of its history had an annual average roster of 100 members and recruited to its ranks French, European, and American Masons residing in Paris. The lodge charter stipulated that there would be active and associate members in the Nine Sisters and that newly elected active members were expected to give before the lodge presentations concerning their contributions either to the arts or to the sciences. This document also provided that assemblies and special meetings of the lodge for the most part should be devoted to cultural operations and that the lodge should award monies from a special fund to members who made outstanding contributions to science, to the humanities, and to the fine arts. According to the constitution, the lodge upon the recommendation of its officers was empowered to fund and to sponsor ancillary cultural institutions.[61]

Leadership played a significant role in fostering the development of the Nine Sisters. A Master, a Secretary, and the Orators served as the major officers of the Nine Sisters and generally speaking were annually elected. Masters of the Nine Sisters were entrusted with the power of conferring rites to candidates and occasionally performed this function. Lodge Masters were responsible for the coordination of the cultural operations of the Nine Sisters and were expected to assist in the recruiting of members. Jerome Lalande and Benjamin Franklin, the first two Masters of the Nine Sisters, staged numerous assemblies and meetings and were quite successful in recruiting Masons from the Paris Academy of Sciences, the Parisian Academy of Painting and Sculpture, the *Académie Française*, and the Salon of Madame Helvétius. The minor enlighteners Beaumont, Dupaty, and Pastoret served as Masters of the Nine Sisters during the 1780s and provided the lodge with minimal administrative direction. These three Masters became personally involved in matters concerning state reforms, but revealed little interest in recruiting new members to the lodge and in holding assemblies and special meetings to promote the cultural activities of the Nine Sisters. Orators of the lodge as well were involved with cultural functions. They were entrusted with the responsibilities of arranging lectures, scientific demonstrations, and artistic displays and of delivering eulogies of eminent enlighteners and Masons. It seemed that friends of Masters of the Nine Sisters were elected as Orators and that Orators for the most part were minor Parisian intellectuals. The Secretary of the lodge was allowed to engage in correspondence with other lodges and was expected to call the roll; he, however, was not obligated to record the minutes of lodge meetings and assemblies. In deciding against taking notes, Gébelin and other Secretaries of the Nine Sisters evidently wished to preserve the secret character of the lodge and unfortunately have provided historians with no information about the inner organizational workings and the cultural operations of this Masonic learned society.[62]

3. Cultural Operations and Special Projects of the Nine Sisters

During his first term as Master between 1776 and 1777, Lalande cautiously governed the lodge and seemed to do little to stimulate its cultural activities. The resignation of Lalande in 1776 as Orator of the Grand Orient and the lack of cultural operations of the Nine Sisters suggested that he evidently was attempting to conciliate his grand lodge opponents. Lalande further directed his attention to the recruitment of members to the Nine Sisters and attracted to its ranks minor Masonic enlighteners connected with important cultural institutions in Paris.

Two founding fathers of the Nine Sisters were scientists. Pierre Le Changeux and Jean Chauvet evidently wished to become involved with the lodge to further their scientific careers. Minimal evidence about the career of Chauvet has been discovered. Chauvet belonged to the Bordeaux Academy of Sciences and was a corresponding member of the Paris Academy of Sciences. He came to Paris in the early 1770s and, upon the suggestion of his friend Lalande, decided to affiliate with the newly established Parisian Masonic learned society. Chauvet contributed nothing of significance either to French science or to the Nine Sisters.[63] Pierre Le Changeux differed from Chauvet, publishing several minor scientific works and assuming a leadership position in the lodge. Le Changeux belonged to the Paris Academy of Sciences and to the Salon of Madame Helvétius, knew Lalande, and in 1776 was elected as an Orator of the Nine Sisters. He was a mechanist and eventually acquired some prominence in the Parisian scientific world. Le Changeux conducted experiments with the barometer, wrote an article about this instrument for the *Journal de Physique*, and in 1781 published *Le Barométrographie et autres machines météorlogiques*.[64]

Most of the founding fathers were writers; many were connected with Parisian literary circles and probably envisioned affiliation with the Nine Sisters as being important for the publicizing of their works. Cailhava, who wrote *L'Egoisme*, and Saint-Firmin, who published *La Jeune Esclave ou les Francais à Tunis*, were playwrights and members of the *Académie française*. Both Masonic dramatists realized that scenes from their plays could be staged during lodge assemblies[65] Fallet and Garnier were two minor poets and evidently thought that their connection with the Nine Sisters would provide them with new literary opportunities. Fallet in 1775 composed "Mes premices" and the next year the heroic poem "Phaeton," while Garnier during the 1770s wrote poems for the *Mercure de France*.[66] It seemed, however, that these two poets never acquired prominence in the Parisian literary world and that their participation in the cultural operations of the Nine Sisters was minimal. Abbé Robin conversely became a significant member of the Nine Sisters. This minor writer published works to defend the principles of the American Revolution, played an active part in lodge projects designed to support leaders of this revolution, and at a later time delivered a lecture to the lodge about Masonic rites.[67]

The induction of Voltaire into the lodge in 1778 was the first major cultural operation of the Nine Sisters and was recognized as being important for several reasons. In light of his affiliation with the Paris Academy of Sciences, Lalande knew Voltaire and evidently in early 1778 was the Mason to convince this eminent enlightener to apply to the Nine Sisters. Lalande realized that the initiation of Voltaire into the Nine Sisters would impress authorities of the Grand Orient and would help to enhance the stature of the Lodge[68] Lalande also realized that numerous Masons would favorably view the lodge as a result of this initiation. Minor Parisian Masonic writers would want to join the Nine Sisters, realizing that they would be given the opportunity of meeting and of even working with the philosopher of Ferney. Lalande probably thought that, motivated by the ideas of Voltaire and by the teachings of the Craft, Parisian Masonic intellectuals from the humanities and sciences would flock to the lodge, would perform significant cultural functions, and thus would help to transform the Nine Sisters into a viable Enlightenment institution. He further believed that the affiliation of Voltaire with the Nine Sisters would prompt Masonic enlighteners from other nations in Europe to become members of the lodge and thus would enable it to evolve into an international Masonic learned society. It also appeared that some enlighteners not affiliated with the Craft would notice the connection of Voltaire with the Nine Sisters and would recognize the cultural importance of this lodge.[69]

Some unusual developments were associated with the induction of Voltaire into the Nine Sisters. Although not a member of the Craft, Voltaire in flagrant violation of Masonic regulations was allowed on March 21, 1778 to attend as a visitor the meeting of the Nine Sisters. After this meeting, the philosopher of Ferney, who evidently enjoyed this session of the lodge, informed Lalande that he would consent to be initiated into the Nine Sisters during its next meeting.[70] The induction ceremonies of Voltaire were held on Tuesday, April 7, 1778 and were not conducted according to stated Masonic procedures. Because of the age and the poor health of the philosopher of Ferney, the Master Lalande was constrained to abbreviate the initiation ceremonies. Leaning on the arm of his guide, Benjamin Franklin, the blindfolded Voltaire was escorted into the lodge chamber and was asked several questions about his moral conduct. Without being required to receive the three mandatory degrees of Blue Lodge Masonry, he was informed of the signs, secrets, and symbols of the Craft and then was proclaimed a member of the order and the Nine Sisters.[71]

During this meeting, more time was devoted to paying tribute to Voltaire than to inducting him into the Nine Sisters. Benjamin Franklin, Count Stroganoff, Dr. Guillotin, and other lodge members extended their congratulations to

Voltaire, and then the minor painter Monnet presented this eminent enlightener with a portrait. After the lodge orchestra played several pieces, Count de Gébelin delivered a short lecture about ancient and modern Masonic ceremonies; Gébelin maintained that, like Voltaire, the ancient and modern ceremonies of the Craft emphasized the importance of the Supreme Creator, natural laws, religious toleration, and natural liberties.[72] Lalande then gave a major speech, explaining the importance of the occasion and assessing from a Masonic perspective the achievements of Voltaire.

> My dear brother, we have marked a great moment in our lodge and have admitted to our ranks an Apollonian and a friend of humanity. We are delighted with your zeal about being admitted to the Nine Sisters and know that you will continue to promote the arts and sciences.... In entering Masonry, know that your efforts should be directed to ending fanaticism and superstition. You have raised a temple to the Eternal and were a Mason in spirit prior to receiving your degrees. You have used the square in your actions and worn the apron during your fruitful career.[73]

To Lalande, the lodge was fortunate to receive into its ranks the indisputable leader of the French Enlightenment and the Party of Humanity. Lalande perceived the accomplishments of Voltaire, the concepts of the Enlightenment, and the teachings of Masonry as being intimately related to each other. To Lalande, members of the Nine Sisters were perceived as disciples of Voltaire and as Masonic enlighteners. Members of the lodge relied upon reason to discover the natural laws of experimental science, revived salient philosophical teachings of the ancients, and utilized literature as a vehicle to encourage the implementation of legal and religious reforms in France.

Approximately seven weeks after his induction into the Nine Sisters, Voltaire on May 30, 1778 died. Similar to other Parisian learned societies, the lodge on November 28, 1778, held a special meeting to pay tribute to this deceased brother. Ninety-five members of the Nine Sisters and 150 Masonic visitors were present during the lodge of mourning directed by Lalande. During this meeting, La Dixmerie delivered the major eulogy, the lodge orchestra played the march from the opera *Alceste*, and the bust of Voltaire done by Houdon was placed on display.[74]

The lodge in 1778 sponsored other cultural activities. A lodge banquet was held in July at Passy to honor Benjamin Franklin. During this session, a plaque containing the silhouettes of Helvétius and Voltaire was presented to this American enlightener, and then theatrical performances were staged.[75] The lodge on

September 30, 1778 held a special banquet to celebrate St. Jerome's Day and to honor its Master, Jerome Lalande. Many speeches were given about his contributions to science. These speeches praised Lalande for publishing *Traité sur la Navigation* and for writing articles in the *Encyclopédie* about Egyptian astronomy and about the manufacturing of paper. In their addresses, members of the lodge also referred to his observations of Venus and to his views about the parallax of the moon.[76] La Dixmerie sang a song in honor of Lalande and well portrayed this Masonic mechanist:

> Do you know in this canton a certain savant and a fine gentleman, who, from study of Copernicus and Newton, wrote a tome? We know him as Monsieur Jerome.
>
> The body that he observed so closely was the planet Venus. All these things are known about this genius.... When he speaks and writes, we applaud him in great chorus....[77]

La Dixmerie as well spoke of the Masonic achievements of this astronomer; he claimed that Lalande helped to develop French Masonry into a significant cultural institution and that his *Mémoire historique sur la Maçonnerie* and his article regarding the order in the 1777 supplement of the *Encyclopédie* well explained the importance of Masonry during the *ancien régime*. Before this session closed, La Dixmerie sadly announced that Lalande was serving his final term as Master of the Nine Sisters[78]

Prior to the conclusion of his third term, Lalande in April 1779 presided over a session to honor the lodge members Vernet and Lemierre. Vernet was a painter, and Lemierre was a writer who was admitted to the *Académie française* two years hence. During this celebration, Cubières presented a brief oration and identified these two Masonic enlighteners with their ancient counterparts.

> Muses, open your temple to these two distinguished artists. One imitated Linnus, the other Zeuxis: One teaches by precepts and writings, the other by his brilliant paintings.[79]

With the departure of Lalande as Master, the lodge needed a prominent Masonic enlightener to direct its cultural operations and thus on May 21, 1779 elected Benjamin Franklin as his successor. Members of the Nine Sisters were certainly familiar with the reputation of Franklin as an enlightener; they knew about his electrical experiments, his invention of the lightning rod, his founding of the

Pennsylvania Academy, and his creation of the American Philosophical Society.[80] As members of the Nine Sisters realized, Franklin was an active Mason. As a young man, he was inducted in 1731 into the St. John's Lodge of Philadelphia, published on his printing press copies of the *Constitutions*, and served in 1749 as Deputy Grand Master of Pennsylvania.[81] While in Paris during the late 1770s to secure financial and military assistance for the Second Continental Congress, Franklin displayed interest in Enlightenment and Masonic activities. He frequently participated in the Salon of Madame Helvétius, met at Auteuil many prominent members of the Nine Sisters, and willingly consented to become involved in the cultural operations of the lodge and to serve as its Master.[82]

During the mastership of Franklin between 1779 and 1780, two major assemblies devoted to cultural activities were held. The activities of August 16, 1779 revolved around literature and the fine arts. Greuze and Houdon arranged an impressive display for this session. Greuze showed his recent paintings of French villages and his portraits of eminent Frenchmen, and Houdon exhibited his busts of Franklin, La Dixmerie, and other lodge members.[83] La Dixmerie, who was reelected as a lodge Orator, gave his *Éloge de Montaigne*, and Roucher read stanzas from his poem "Novembre." In this poem, he explained to members of the lodge the importance of state reforms and encouraged them to work for their implementation.[84] After the reading of this poem, Abbé Robin delivered a lecture concerning the relationship between ancient literature and Masonic rites. In presenting to the lodge important ideas from his *Recherches sur les initiations anciennes et modernes*, published in 1779, Robin claimed that important myths and legends of Egyptian, Greek, and Roman literature constituted the foundations of Modern Speculative Freemasonry.[85]

The cultural operations of this assembly and those of the May 1, 1780 session revealed that the Nine Sisters would function as a center for Masonic supporters of the American Revolution. These activities flagrantly violated Masonic regulations, but for unknown reasons were never questioned by Grand Orient authorities. The cultural operations encouraged by Franklin conversely permitted the lodge and French Masonry to become identified with this American and political cultural movement. During the August assembly, Hilliard d'Auberteuil read the preface of his *Essais historiques et politiques sur les Anglo-Americains*, one of the first works about America to appear in France.[86] In the preface of this detailed work composed from newspaper accounts, d'Auberteuil perceives Americans as advocates of natural liberties and virtue; he further is impressed with the operations of American state assemblies and with American efforts to detach themselves from the British monarchy.[87]

> State assemblies are elected and are designed to operate for the welfare of their citizens.... Most state legislatures are empowered to collect taxes and to levy monies for state projects....
>
> Americans are fighting against the tyranny of the English king and nation. This nation has enslaved her American colonies economically and politically. If these virtuous colonies are to end this enslavement by George III and his minister Pitt, French assistance is needed.... Since 1763, the English have dominated the economic and political institutions of the American colonies and Canada and have posed a threat to the French colonies of Guadeloupe and Martinique....[88]

D'Auberteuil admired the constitutions of New York, Pennsylvania and Virginia. The constitutions of these three states embodied the republican principles of the separation of powers, of legislative representation, and of freedom of speech, press, and religion.[89] D'Auberteuil as well was present during the lodge feast of May 1780. He gave a lecture about the contributions of Franklin and Washington to the American Revolution and maintained that these two Masons had activated the principles of the Enlightenment and those of the Craft. After this speech, John Paul Jones was honored by members of the Nine Sisters and received tribute from La Dixmerie for "his meritorious service and heroic deeds."[90]

After the mastership of Franklin, members of the Nine Sisters still continued to display interest in America and during two sessions in 1785 engaged in significant cultural activities. During the mastership of the obscure lawyer Elie de Beaumont, a Lodge of Mourning was convened on March 7, 1785 to honor the memory of the Americanophile and lodge Secretary Court de Gébelin. As a tribute to him, Roucher, the new Secretary of the lodge, read his ode entitled "L'Immortalité de l'homme." This ode confirmed the Masonic belief concerning the afterlife and referred to the sprig of acacia.

> Man knows that at the end of life on Earth, the spirit separates from the body and seeks its destiny in heaven.... There a Voice informs the immortal soul of its triumphant earthly glories....[91]

A lodge assembly was convened in June to honor Franklin prior to his return to the United States. Louis Alexandre, the Duke of Rochefoucauld d'Anville presented to the lodge his translations of American republican writings; the duke distributed to lodge members copies of the Declaration of Independence, the Articles of Confederation, and six state constitutions. Rochefoucauld maintained that these documents well explained concepts concerning natural liberties, bicameralism, unicameralism, and the separation of powers and in his view were considered as major contributions to the political thought of the Enlightenment.[92] Before this assembly terminated, Houdon displayed his marble statue of Washington, and Beaumont announced that the lodge would offer a prize of 600 *livres* for the best paper on the topic of "Benjamin Franklin *vivant.*"[93]

It appeared to be unusual that with the exception of these two meetings, the lodge between 1781 and 1789 held no other assemblies for the staging of cultural events. Administrators of the Grand Orient perhaps discouraged officers of the Nine Sisters from holding assemblies and were worried that the activities of the Nine Sisters might revolve around French political problems and consequently would pose a threat to the monarchy. The election of minor enlighteners as Masters of the Nine Sisters during this decade also appeared to be related to the lack of cultural operations of the lodge. The Masters Milly, Dupaty, Beaumont, and Pastoret were not of the stature of Lalande and Franklin and were not that well known in Parisian cultural circles. Dupaty, Beaumont, and Pastoret were proponents of state reforms, but did not hold lodge assemblies to propagandize the cause of reform.[94] These three Masters continued, however, to promote the special projects of the lodge.

Members of the lodge financed and edited *Affaires de l'Angleterre et de l'Amérique*. Edited by Jean Robinet, Rochefoucauld, and Gébelin, this journal was published between 1776 and 1780 and was intended to furnish news about the War of Independence and to support the cause of the American revolutionaries. The journal contained descriptive accounts about military and political developments in America and summaries of political events in England and in France. The volumes of *Affaires* also contained an occasional editorial and many translations of important American political documents. By publishing the Declaration of Independence and the constitutions of several American states, the Masonic editors of this journal succeeded in revealing to their French subscribers American perceptions of natural liberties and of republican institutions. After securing diplomatic recognition and financial assistance from Louis XVI, Franklin during his second term as Master of the Nine Sisters convinced the editors of this journal to terminate its publication.[95]

Support of the Nine Sisters was extended to the Gallo-American Society. A member of the lodge, Brissot de Warville established this society in 1787 with the intention of fostering mutual understanding and commercial relations between America and France. The society succeeded in encouraging a few Parisian Masons to purchase land in America and in stimulating several lodge members to write articles about American society. This society however was ephemeral and with the outbreak of the French Revolution no longer functioned.[96]

The operations of educational institutions sponsored by the Nine Sisters were more successful than those of the Gallo-American Society. Masonic and Enlightenment ideas explained why the lodge decided to operate schools. Members of the Nine Sisters believed that orders of the Catholic Church dominated French education and that the state should fund and control the educational system. They further believed that state schools should be open to the public, should be inexpensive, and should place emphasis upon the humanities and sciences. In recognizing that the French Crown had done little to promote public education and that a valuable need would be filled, Franklin recommended that the lodge should allocate funds for the creation and the maintenance of a school. After the members of the lodge approved this proposal, Franklin on November 17, 1780 announced the opening of the Apollonian Society. This school was open to the public and offered inexpensive courses. Many members of the Nine Sisters were involved with the Apollonian Society; Gébelin frequently lectured about linguistics and ancient philosophy. The teaching of ancient music by Rozier and that of European literature by La Dixmerie suggested that the Apollonian Society emphasized the importance of courses in the liberal arts. Prior to closing its doors in 1781, the society also published a journal which probably contained significant lectures given by members of the Nine Sisters who taught in the school.[97]

The lodge during the 1780s sponsored two *musées*. A *musée* under the direction of Gébelin was opened in late 1781 and, similar to the Apollonian Society, offered an envisaging program in the humanities; students attending the *musée* took ancient philosophy from Gébelin, European literature from Saint-Firmin, and French drama from Cailhava. This *musée* held several special events. It sponsored lectures, displayed many busts sculptured by Houdon, and honored Benjamin Franklin for negotiating the 1783 Treaty of Paris.[98] The lodge in 1782 opened a second *musée* and after the death of Gébelin decided in 1784, probably for financial reasons, to merge the operations of both schools. Officers of the lodge appointed Pilâtre de Rozier to supervise the operations of the newly created *Musée de Paris*. This school was designed to promote the arts, sciences, and commerce and offered a wide selection of courses. Students took physics from Sue and chemistry from Fourcroy.[99] Students enrolled in scientific courses were granted permission to utilize the facilities of the Paris Academy of Sciences. The *Musée de Paris* also offered courses in mathematics, in anatomy and physiology, in geography, in ancient and modern literature, and in textile manufacturing. After the death of Rozier in 1785, this school was closed.[100]

In 1785 the lodge established the *Lycée de Paris* to replace the *musée* of Rozier. The *lycée* was known for offering extensive programs in the arts and sciences to male and female students. This school also was known for its well qualified faculty; Condorcet, Fourcroy, La Harpe, and Marmontel held chairs in the *lycée*. This institution operated until the outbreak of the French Revolution and proved to be a successful project sponsored by the lodge.[101]

C. The Cultural Functions of Enlighteners of the Nine Sisters

1. Mechanists of the Nine Sisters

There were not many mechanists associated with the Nine Sisters. Several physicians belonged to the lodge. While the cultural activities and projects of the Nine Sisters were not directly related to medicine, physicians retained their affiliation with the lodge and evidently were interested in the various facets of its Enlightenment operations. The lack of astronomers and physicists in the Nine Sisters certainly was related to the shift of interest from mechanistic to materialistic concepts and paradigms.[102] While not presenting many papers or experiments during lodge assemblies, some mechanists, however, supported projects of the lodge and taught in its schools.

Chabanneau was one of the few physicists to belong to the lodge. He was a minor physicist, not holding membership in any important scientific society and evidently perceiving affiliation with the Nine Sisters as being important to his career. Chabanneau during the early 1780s taught in Paris, was admitted to the Nine Sisters, and became friendly with the Masonic and Spanish enlightener Count Pena Florida. As a result of the efforts of Pena Florida, Chabanneau in 1785 was granted a chair in physics in the University of Madrid and five years later published in Spanish a comprehensive work concerning significant eighteenth century discoveries in physics.[103]

The astronomer Jean Bailly affiliated with the Nine Sisters for several reasons. He belonged to the Paris Academy of Sciences and knew Lalande. The occasional visits of Bailly to the Salon of Madame Helvétius also suggested his connection to an important circle of the Nine Sisters and helped to explain why he became friendly with Roucher and Gébelin. Like these two officers of the Nine Sisters and other members of the lodge, Bailly subscribed to deistic ideas. He believed that the study of ancient astronomy and mythology would reveal pertinent insights about the attributes of the Supreme Creator and about His relationship to Nature and to man.[104]

Bailly became an important contributor to the astronomy of the French Enlightenment. In 1759 he determined the orbit of Halley's Comet and in the following year determined from his observatory in Paris the positions of Mars, Jupiter, and Saturn. In cooperation with his friend and teacher Lacaille, he also observed in 1760 the transit of Venus—a development enabling a more accurate measurement of the parallax of the Sun.[105] Five years later, Bailly delivered lectures to members of the Paris Academy of Sciences about the moons of Jupiter and in detail described their inclinations and nodes.[106]

Cardinal ideas of Bailly appeared in *Histoire de l'astronomie ancienne*. In this work published in 1775, he maintains that the ancient Egyptians, Chinese and Greeks shared similar astronomical views; astronomers of these ancient civilizations devised lunar and solar calendars, made records of lunar eclipses, identified seven planets of the solar system, and offered speculations about the distances between the Earth and the fixed stars.[107] In this history, Bailly claims that ancient astronomers and philosophers became advocates of the great order and advanced myths to explain how the universe, Nature, and man functioned. He describes some important myths. Prosperine is known for living both above and below the Earth and symbolizes the appearance of the Sun in the morning and its disappearance in the evening. The struggle between Hercules and the Amazons represents the conflict between the forces of light and those of darkness. The tales of Adonis and Osiris reveal the themes of life, death, and resurrection.[108] As attested to by these and other myths, the ancients, according to Bailly, believed that moral and natural laws were closely interrelated to each other and were to be traced to a Single Cause.

The several physicians of the Nine Sisters believed that clinical and pathological studies would help in determining mechanistic principles relating to the operations of the body. These doctors further worked to improve facilities of Parisian hospitals and to promote the public health movement in the French capital.[109] Victor de Seze was a minor Parisian physician connected with the circle of Guillotin and espoused mechanistic ideas. In *Recherches philosophiques sur la sensibilité ou la vie animale*, published in 1786, De Seze maintains that physicians should investigate and classify body organs and sensations in light of their functions.[110] While known for his device for decapitation, Dr. Joseph Guillotin made other significant contributions to Parisian medicine and Masonry. He served as one of the founders of the French Academy of Medicine, was appointed as a regent of the University of Paris Medical School, and played an active role during the 1780s in attempting to improve the conditions of hospitals in the French capital. Guillotin as well denounced Mesmer and his followers as quacks and believed that they would thwart the advancement of Parisian clinical medicine. He identified Masonry as a reform institution, served as master of the Parisian Lodge *Concorde Fraternelle*, but was not actively involved in the cultural operations and projects of the Nine Sisters.[111]

Like many members of the lodge, Dr. Pierre Jean George Cabanis was an intellectually versatile individual. Cabanis was interested in ancient literature and in 1777 was honored by the *Académie française* for his French translation of *The Iliad*. He further during the late 1770s earned his medical degree, became the "adopted son" of Madame Helvétius, and gave frequent lectures in her salon about the sensationalistic philosophy of John Locke.[112] As a result of his friendships with Lalande, with Franklin, and with other Masons of this salon, Cabanis in 1779 decided to affiliate with the Nine Sisters. He envisioned the lodge as being a significant institution for the promotion of his medical ideas.

The philosophy of Cabanis was significant to Parisian medical thought; he believed that inductive techniques and sense observations were essential for the proper practice of medicine.

> Until the appearance of Sydenham, inductive techniques in medicine were unknown. This seventeenth century English physician gave to medicine the true spirit of observation. Locke adhered to the observational techniques of Sydenham.... Locke showed that babies at birth have a clear mind and in light of their sense observations acquire knowledge....[113]

To Cabanis, medicine as well was indebted to the natural philosophy of Newton, utilizing its "precise language and reasoning procedures for the examination of the parts of the body and for the treatment of diseases."[114] According to this medical philosopher, clinical investigations enabled numerous French physicians to discover new remedies for diseases.[115] Cabanis maintains that clinical studies enabled physiologists to classify organs and parts of the body and to explain digestion, muscular movements, and the functioning of nerves and veins. According to Cabanis, French physicians probed the mind and explained its operations in light of sense impressions.[116]

2. The Materialists of the Lodge

Numerous proponents of materialism affiliated with the Nine Sisters. Most materialists of the lodge held membership in the Paris Academy of Sciences and belonged to the circles of Fourcroy and Rozier. Some materialists offered courses in schools sponsored by the Nine Sisters. Materialists for the most part wished to utilize the lodge as a vehicle for the promotion of their chemical writings.

Antoine Fourcroy made significant contributions to late eighteenth century French chemistry. His *Elémens* served as one of the major texts of inorganic chemistry during the late eighteenth century and contained many and varying experiments regarding metals, acids, alkalis, and salts.[117] A member of the Paris Academy of Sciences, Fourcroy in 1777 delivered to this society a lecture concerning the reaction of iron salts to alkalis and acids. He maintained that iron salts reacted more to acids than to alkalis and that upon exposure to acids, these salts emitted an inflammable gas.[118] As Fourcroy explained to members of the academy, these experiments suggested that iron ores could be decomposed. In other experiments, he ascertained the properties of gold, silver, platinum, and mercury and showed that when mixed with strong acids, these chemicals were difficult to decompose.[119] Fourcroy also studied human blood. He succeeded in determining the properties of blood and advanced the view that additional chemical investigations of this substance might lead to an understanding of the causes of various diseases.[120]

The Englishman John Forster, who spent considerable time in Paris during the 1780s, and Claude Berthollet were connected with the circle of Fourcroy. The influence of Fourcroy evidently explained why both of these chemists chose to affiliate with the Nine Sisters and why Cadet de Vaux, a lodge member and an editor of *Journal de Paris*, decided to publish some of their experiments.[121] Berthollet performed valuable experiments concerning bleaching and dyeing. He demonstrated that if placed in a tub of muriatic acid, cloth containing vegetable colors would be bleached.

> When vegetable colors are immersed in oxygenated muriatic acid, they are completely destroyed. A mixture of different colors, in a similar exposure, suffers from the same change.... We may conclude that the coloring vegetable matters, which have been acted upon and deprived of their properties of producing color, have taken away the oxygen from the acid by a strong chemical attraction, and have, by means of this combination, acquired new properties, whilst they have lost that of producing color....[122]

Berthollet and Forster believed that experiments would lead to an understanding of some chemical compounds and would demonstrate their usefulness. Forster developed methods for assaying metals. He performed experiments with iron ores and showed that when exposed to fire, iron could be separated from compounds and could be used for industrial purposes. The experiments of Forster further demonstrated that substances could be classified into four groups: earths, salts, metals, and gases.[123]

Joseph and Jacques Montgolfier belonged to the Nine Sisters and the Paris Academy of Sciences, were members of the scientific circle of Rozier, and demonstrated that heated gases could propel their aerostatic balloon. The Montgolfiers in 1782 conducted experiments concerning the density of heated air and concluded that an object filled with hot air could rise from the surface of the Earth. On June 5, 1783, they gave a public demonstration of their machine. When inflated with hot air and released, their aerostatic machine, made of paper and approximately thirty-five feet in diameter, ascended to a height of about 6,000 feet and descended gradually as the air in it cooled. As a result of the excitement aroused by this flight, Louis XVI insisted that the Montgolfiers present a demonstration of their invention to the royal family. With animals as its passengers, the aerostatic balloon on September 19, 1783 was released at Versailles, ascended to a height of 1,500 feet, and then fell to the ground without injuring its passengers.[124]

Rozier wished to experiment with the machine of his two friends. He was a minor scientist in Paris during the 1780s and was known for teaching chemistry to ladies, for inventing the phosphoric candle, and for experimenting with hydrogen. Rozier in October 1783 offered his services to the Montgolfiers and evidently recognized that he could acquire fame for being the first person in history to make a successful flight in an aerostatic balloon. Rozier that year made two successful ascents, rising on October 15th to a height of eighty-three feet. During his second ascent on November 21st, Rozier was accompanied by the Marquis d'Arlandes, remained in the air for twenty-five minutes, crossed the Seine at 3,000 feet, and descended safely having completed a trip of six miles. After several ascents in 1784, Rozier was convinced that he could direct a flight across the English Channel. In an effort to accomplish this objective, he was launched in an aerostatic balloon on June 16, 1785 and reached a height of 1,700 feet. Rozier then encountered problems with fire, crashed the balloon several miles from Boulogne, and was instantly killed.[125]

3. Neoclassicism and the Nine Sisters

Members of the Nine Sisters associated with the humanities and the fine arts shared in common several important beliefs; they believed that the revival of ancient ideologies and paradigms would enable them to become modern enlighteners. These enlighteners concentrated their efforts on portraying the features of

Nature and the qualities of man and probably realized the importance of Masonic teachings regarding the ancients and Nature. Many of these enlighteners actively participated in the assemblies of the Nine Sisters and were provided with splendid opportunities to read their poems, to stage scenes from their plays, and to exhibit their paintings and statuary. Most of these savants of the lodge held membership in Parisian learned societies and belonged to varying cultural circles in the French capital.

Artists of the Nine Sisters identified major concepts of the ancients with themes of naturalism. Many of these artists became known for their vivid portrayals of ancient and modern leaders and society. Many painters of the lodge as well belonged to the French Royal Academy of Painting. Claude Notté belonged to this society and acquired prominence as a portrait painter. Notté did portraits of Franklin, Milly, Dupaty, and other modern enlighteners of the lodge. Claude Vernet painted a few portraits, but was elected to the Royal Academy of Painting as a result of other works. Vernet conveyed themes of naturalism in his paintings of French port cities, rivers, farms, and forests.[126]

Jean Greuze was recognized as the most noted artist in the Nine Sisters. After studying in a studio in Lyon, Greuze in 1747 at age twenty-two moved to Paris, became known for *Un Écolier endormi sur son livre* and for *Portrait de M. Sylvestre* and consequently in 1755 was elected to the Royal Academy of Painting.[127] He became involved in the salon life of Paris during the 1760s and painted several important portraits. In *Comte d'Angivillers*, Greuze superbly depicted the cold and stern qualities of this French noble. Praise was offered in 1765 for *La Mère Bien-Aimée*; this work well conveyed the half-open mouth, the swimming eyes, and the relaxed position of the subject.[128] He also painted in 1765 *Sévère et Caracalla* which showed Severus reproaching his son for attempting to assassinate him. Greuze during the 1770s painted two portraits of members of the Nine Sisters; he did colorful portraits of Benjamin Franklin and Count Stroganoff.[129] Some of the paintings of Greuze during the late 1770s revealed astute perceptions of French society. In *L'Accordée de Village*, Greuze portrayed the life of French peasants and exhibited concern for their plight. In *The Death of the Paralytic*, Greuze recreated the scene of a dying middle class man and in cleverly using colors conveyed the ruefulness expressed by the immediate members of the family.[130]

Features of naturalism were embodied in the sculpture of Jean Antoine Houdon. In addition to doing busts of American Revolutionary heroes, he sculptured statues of French enlighteners involved with the Nine Sisters. Ancient and modern legal expressions and symbols appeared in his statues of Dupaty and Pastoret and suggested his concern for the cause of natural liberties. Perceived as the modern Phidias, Houdon sculptured an enormous statue of Jerome Lalande, portraying this Masonic astronomer as he viewed the heavens with his telescope.[131]

The few musicians of the Nine Sisters belonged to the Royal Academy of Music and expressed interest in the ideas of the ancients. They were involved with the lodge orchestra, staged several operas based on ancient legends, and during lodge assemblies gave musical renditions of ancient lyrics. Nicolas Piccinni served as conductor of the lodge orchestra and became a spokesman for dramatic opera. He believed that the legends and heroes of ancient civilizations should be emphasized in a modern operatic setting. Piccinni was known for revising the operas *Atys* and *Didon* to conform to his standards and presented to the lodge select acts from these two works. The singing of Pierre Tirot and Jean Lays and the violin solos of Pierre Lahoussaye were featured to dramatize the themes of these operas.[132] Like Piccinni, John Palza and Charles Turschmidt served as conductors of the lodge orchestra, composed several minor pieces, and in 1786 left Paris to accept positions in the orchestra of Frederick William II. The departure of these two conductors and the lack of musicians in the Nine Sisters suggested that the lodge did not develop into a major center of Parisian music.[133]

Minor Parisian poets belonged to the lodge and displayed great interest in the ideas and models of their ancient counterparts. Most of these poets participated in Parisian salons and evidently envisioned the Lodge of the Nine Sisters as another cultural agency enabling them to reveal their literary talents. Some of these poets were given the opportunity to read eulogies and lyrics during lodge assemblies. Others attended meetings of the lodge as interested observers, but were known in Paris for stimulating interest in ancient ideas through their translations. Jacques Delille was educated in the classics and translated into French the "Georgics" of Vergil. Voltaire regarded this translation as one of the finest works in French literature. Indicative of his interest in the ancients, Delille also rendered a translation of the "Aeneid" and wrote the poem "L'Homme des Champs ou les Georgiques françaises."[134] Louis Fontanes believed that many poems of Alexander Pope contained significant ideas of the ancients. Fontanes in 1783 translated into French "An Essay on Man."[135] He further composed in 1778 "Forét de Navarre" and in this poem praised the ancients for their views concerning Nature.[136]

Jean Roucher wrote "Les Mois" in 1779 and explains in this poem that ancient and modern enlighteners were involved in the study of Nature. He pays tribute to ancient Greek and Roman natural philosophers and to Newton.

Roucher maintains that the laws of Newton enabled modern enlighteners to explain the systematic operations of Nature.

> Before Newton, Nature concealed her laws.... Newton made the heavens his domain and through his discoveries made the world humane.... All men can understand his system, for gravity, motion, and attraction serve as the basis of the solar system.... Attest then to the honor and the glory of his work.... Oh, man and Nature be indebted to this genius....[137]

Like Roucher, the obscure Masonic poet Barthelemy Imbert perceived the importance of the contributions of Newton to the Enlightenment. Imbert offered praise to Newton and to French enlighteners in "L'Utilité des découverts dans les sciences et dans les arts sous le regne de Louis XV."[138]

Francois Turpin and Constantin Volney, who did not play an active role in the activities of the lodge, were known in Paris for their works concerning political and cultural developments in ancient history. Members of the Nine Sisters perceived Turpin as the Plutarch of eighteenth century France.[139] Turpin was in fact a minor enlightener, and little evidence has been discovered about his career. He published in 1769 *Histoire du gouvernement des anciennes républiques* and envisioned ancient monarchs as being capable administrators. To Turpin, these monarchs selected qualified advisers, did not usurp the powers of legislatures, and assisted the courts in promoting justice.[140] Turpin and Volney viewed ancient history somewhat differently. An active participant in the Salon of Madame Helvétius, Volney, like Gébelin and other members of this circle, emphasizes in *Les Ruines* the importance of ancient myths. Volney maintains that Egyptian priests and Greek and Roman philosophers developed myths to explicate the operations of Nature and the concepts of civic morality. He also believes that the decline of cultural and moral values led to the demise and to the eventual collapse of the political and economic institutions of ancient civilizations.[141]

The works of Gébelin concerning ancient language, myths, and mystery cults revealed the efforts of this minor enlightener to promote the study of linguistics and anthropology. In *Histoire Naturelle De La Parole*, published in 1776, Gébelin explains salient functions of language. He maintains that humans were endowed by the Creator with the ability to speak and thus differed from animals. To Gébelin, humans utilized language to reveal their thoughts and sentiments.

> God gave man those organs necessary to speak. Speech is the painting of our ideas and constitutes the essence and glory of man. Animals and men eat,

drink, and sleep, but only men through speech can convey their pleasures, pains, and thoughts.[142]

He maintains that language allowed individuals to understand the operations of Nature and to engage in the study of the arts and sciences. Gébelin also believes that language was needed to permit humans to function in society and to achieve their material and moral objectives through secular and cultural institutions.[143]

> Language enables humans to express ideas derived from hearing, seeing, smelling, and touching.... Words convey ideas and thoughts about the beauties in Nature and in the heavens.... Speech allows individuals to express their thoughts about experiences in society....[144]

Monde Primitif was the voluminous dictionary published by Gébelin in 1773 and contained detailed explanations about words from varying ancient languages. In this work, Gébelin cogently demonstrates that the origins and meanings of words were related to specific functions performed in ancient civilizations. He as well shows that the meanings of words reflected significant cultural concepts, morals, and social values of ancient civilizations.

> Language and words provide the anthropologist with an understanding of the functions of a specific society. Social customs, cultural heritage, and scientific discoveries of a civilization are revealed through the study of language and words....[145]

In this dictionary, Gébelin examines nouns, verbs, and adjectives from Chinese, Hebrew, Greek, and Latin; he develops an etymological scheme to classify ancient words and to compare their meanings. Words are categorized according to their universal meanings, to their nuances, and to their prefixes and suffixes.

> The Greeks developed the study of etymology. They studied the meanings and the structure of ancient words and showed that the meanings of words were associated with the knowledge of Nature.... The Greeks discovered that words from Egyptian, Hebraic, and Chinese civilizations conveyed similar meanings.... The knowledge of ancient words thus contributed to the development of the arts and sciences....[146]

Monde Primitif contained a lengthy account about the Eleusinian Mystery Cult. Gébelin recognizes that this ancient cult and Modern Masonry possessed similarities; both societies performed valuable cultural functions, conveying in their rites important moral doctrines and cultural values of ancient civilizations. Both societies as well functioned as cohesive communities and admitted into their ranks enlighteners.[147]

> The sacred rites of the Eleusinian Mystery Cult were administered with great pomp and embodied cultural ideals cherished in ancient empires. The Eleusinian Mysteries served as a rallying point for the ancients and emphasized the beliefs of virtue, justice, and human liberty....[148]

Gébelin explains activities pertaining to the conferring of the Eleusinian rites in Greece. Prior to his entry into this ancient cult, the initiate pledged that he would aspire to purify his soul and to lead a virtuous life. As an indication of his desire to cleanse his soul, the candidate submerged himself in a river near the plains of Attica; he then received a wreath of flowers, a symbol of the purity of Nature. The candidate proceeded to the Temple of the Gods, went to its altar, and drank a glass of wine. Hierophant, the head priest administering the Eleusinian mysteries, told him that wine symbolized the fertility of the Earth. Hierophant then offered prayers to the Supreme Being, the Sun, and the Earth and explained to the candidate the secrets of the cult. This priest escorted the new member of the order to the banquet hall and ended the lengthy ceremonies with a feast.

> The Eleusinian Mysteries revealed the fecundity of Nature and agriculture and symbolized the prosperity of ancient civilizations.... Candidates were required to acknowledge the Attributes of the Supreme Creator and the powers of the Earth and other heavenly bodies. Candidates recognized the importance of the forces of Nature and of the harmony of bodies moving in the heavens....[149]

In light of his studies regarding ancient civilizations, Gébelin became a proponent of the great order. He believed that the ancients established similar secular institutions, developed similar languages, and endorsed similar cultural and moral teachings. Gébelin maintained that like modern enlighteners, those in the ancient world advanced theories to explain how the universe, Nature, and man were interrelated to each other. To Gébelin, the ancients and the moderns were deists and realized that an Omnipotent Spirit governs the operations of the great order.[150]

4. Perceptions of Lodge Members of America

Some writers of the Nine Sisters envisioned America as a utopia of the Enlightenment and belonged to the Americanophile faction of the lodge. Many writers of this group were recruited from the Salon of Madame Helvétius and directly supported lodge operations to popularize the cause of the American Revolution. Several members of the American faction however only wrote about this nation.

Abbé Robin was known for participating in Americanophile activities of the lodge and for writing *Nouveau voyage dans l'Amérique Septentrionale*. In this work published in 1782, Robin perceives America as a major center of the Enlightenment. He maintains that the colleges of this nation and the American Philosophical Society significantly contributed to the arts and sciences and that reason motivated Americans to make new discoveries about the operations of Nature. Robin lauds American political institutions for functioning in light of precisely defined constitutional principles and for protecting natural liberties. He also equates the commercial activities conducted in American cities with material progress.[151]

> The commerce of Bostonians consisted of a variety of articles and was extensive prior to the outbreak of the American Revolution. Bostonians supplied England with timber, codfish, beef, and turpentine. The town has a superb wharf which extends two thousand feet into the sea and which permits the city to have a large amount of commerce....[152]

The views of Brissot de Warville about America resembled those of Robin. Brissot in *Nouveau Voyage* regards this nation as a paradise of the Enlightenment. To Brissot, America consisted of reasonable and virtuous citizens and served as a mecca of republicanism and science. He further perceives Philadelphia as the nucleus of the American Enlightenment.[153]

> Philadelphia may be considered as the major metropolis of the United States. It is certainly the finest town and the best built in America; it is the most wealthy, although not the most luxurious. You find here men of great political and scientific knowledge....[154]

There were other American propagandists in the lodge. Jean Démeunier was known for his French translations of American writings and for his *Essai sur les États-Unis*. Démeunier in this work emphasizes the achievements of state legislatures in America, maintaining that these bodies consisted of elected representatives, enacted laws to guarantee the economic, political, and religious rights of their citizens, and asserted their position against the English crown.[155] The dramatist Sébastien Chamfort reveals in *La Jeune Indienne* his interest in America. In this play, Chamfort presents portrayals of Indians, merchants, and Quakers; he perceives these three groups as being advocates of the concepts of American liberalism.[156] After the *Académie française* staged a performance of this play, Chamfort told Franklin that "America was the place in the universe where the rights of man are best understood."[157]

5. Lodge Proponents of State Reforms

Several members of the Nine Sisters hoped that France would become a nation in which the inalienable rights of man could be respected. Spokesmen of state reforms from the Nine Sisters were familiar with American republican and natural rights ideologies and certainly believed that some American doctrines could be applied to improve conditions in France. These Masonic advocates of reform were not connected, however, with the Salon of Madame Helvétius. They envisioned their affiliation with the lodge as being essential for the dissemination of their views, but were not involved either with any important Parisian cultural groups or with any monarchical institutions. These Masonic enlighteners exhibited minimal interest in the physiocratic views of the royal minister Turgot, but championed major reform proposals of Voltaire and those of the Milanese *philosophe* Beccaria and thus helped to promote the concepts of a civic morality.

It was evident that in light of their views regarding religious toleration, Louis Sebastian Mercier and Elie de Beaumont drank from the same bottle as their Masonic brother Voltaire. Mercier was a minor Parisian satirist and became known for his *L'an deux mille quatre cent quarante*. In this work published in 1771, he maintains that Frenchmen should do penance for the St. Bartholomew's Day Massacre and for the revocation of the Edict of Nantes. Mercier further claims that Louis XV should recognize the religious and civil liberties of the Huguenots and that their emancipation was required for the improvement of French banking and commerce.[158] The persecution of the Huguenot Jean Calas disturbed Beaumont. A minor Parisian trial lawyer, Beaumont published in 1762 *Memoire pour les Calas* and argues that "an innocent man had been convicted and executed because of religious prejudice."[159] He as well implored Louis XV to end the religious and civil disabilities of French Protestants. The commitment of Beaumont to the cause of reform well explained why he became involved in the Nine Sisters. This disciple of Voltaire and Master of the lodge, however, never wrote another work about state reforms, appeared to be frightened of Grand Orient and royal authorities, and consequently decided against holding lodge assemblies to advance the reform movement.

A Master of the lodge, Dupaty wrote about legal reforms, and his problems with the crown justified the concerns of Beaumont. Dupaty served in the Bordeaux *Parlement* between approximately 1768 and 1774 and at this time distinguished himself as a writer. He wrote a eulogy dedicated to L'Hopital and was elected to the La Rochelle Academy. Dupaty in 1774 left Bordeaux to reside in Paris and three years later issued a French translation of *Dei delitti e delle pene* by Beccaria. Major views advanced in this work were important to Dupaty. He like Beccaria believed that criminals were entitled to fair trials, that punishments should be determined in light of the severity of crimes, and that prison conditions should be improved.[160] The year 1785 was a significant one for this Masonic spokesman of reform. Dupaty served as Master of the Nine Sisters, published *Réflexions sur le Droit criminel*, and in light of pressure from royal officials who disapproved of the views advanced in this work, was constrained to leave France and to reside in Italy for approximately a year. He criticized the crown in *Réflexions*, arguing that trial procedures of French courts were unjust, that criminal laws and punishments were stern, and that Louis XVI displayed minimal concern about implementing legal reforms. After his return to France, the obstinate Dupaty refused to alter his position regarding legal reforms; the Rouen *Parlement* arrested, tried, and convicted him for treason. Before receiving his sentence, Dupaty in September 1788 died, believing that "the French *Parlements* lacked dignity, honesty, and tolerance."[161]

Claude Pastoret served as Master of the Nine Sisters between 1786 and 1789 and wrote to vindicate the cause of legal reforms. This Parisian lawyer during the early 1780s issued short works about Zoroaster, Confucius, Mohammed, and Voltaire. Pastoret perceived these philosophers as enlighteners and as advocates of justice.[162] While serving as Master of the Nine Sisters, Pastoret was writing *Des Loix Pénales* and in 1790 published it. He maintains in this work that the legal institutions of ancient Greece and Rome functioned according to principles of justice and that legal and penal systems of modern France were degenerate. Pastoret exhibited concern for Frenchmen accused and convicted of crimes.

> The condemnation of the innocent is unfair. Until a judgment of condemnation is rendered, a defendant is considered innocent. Proof against the accused must be accurate and decisive. If the accused is proven guilty, the punishment should be equivalent to and not greater than the crime. Punishments should be just, constructive and useful. Punishments should be assigned for rehabilitative purposes....[163]

In *Des Loix Pénales*, he calls for the termination of cruel punishments in France. Pastoret condemns the cutting of feet, the mutilation of ears and noses, and the throwing of bodies into scalding water. He implores Louis XVI and French representatives in the National Assembly to end inhumane techniques of capital punishment: flogging until death, burning in the public square, and decapitation.[164] Pastoret further believes that capital punishment for minor crimes was wrong and was excessively used in France and that the French king and legislature, similar to those in ancient history, should be empowered to grant pardons.[165]

Most members of the Nine Sisters probably agreed with the reform proposals advanced in *Des Loix Pénales* and realized that Pastoret during his mastership discreetly managed the affairs of the lodge; they knew that the paucity of lodge meetings during the late 1780s was related to pertinent developments occurring in France. Members of the Nine Sisters realized that with the eruption of the French Revolution, the lodge eventually might be forced to cease its operations.

> As spring gives way to the heat of summer and to the harvest of the fall, the muses of our lodge await the opportunity to relive their golden years....[166]

D. The French Revolution and the Disappearance of the Nine Sisters

Such proved to be the case. During the heat of revolution, the lodge found it difficult to function. The lodge by early 1790 significantly decreased its activities; this body discontinued funding the *lycée* and staged few sessions. The attitudes of lodge members towards the Nine Sisters explained why lodge meetings were infrequently conducted. Most members were concerned about the affairs of the French Revolution and not about those of the Nine Sisters.[167] Other members did not want to become involved in the revolution and refused to attend meetings of the Nine Sisters. They believed that their participation in the lodge would result in attacks from political and anti-Masonic authorities.

Administrators of the Grand Orient first tried to justify the operations of the lodge and then decided to terminate them. Officers of the Grand Orient changed in late 1790 the name of the lodge to the *Société Nationale des Neuf Soeurs*. This action was taken to demonstrate to leaders of the National Assembly that the society was involved with cultural and social activities rather than with political matters.[168] The Grand Orient even permitted this new society to hold open meetings, but discovered that former members of the Nine Sisters were not interested in its activities. In recognizing that the few sessions of the *Société Nationale des Neuf Soeurs* were poorly attended and that the Jacobins, who viewed the Craft as a threat to their regime, would act to suspend Masonic activities, officers of the Grand Orient in November 1792 issued an edict to dissolve this society and thus to end "the golden age of the muses."[169]

Even before the French Revolution, both achievements and failures characterized the operations of the Lodge of the Nine Sisters. In light of major organizational functions of the lodge, its members made some contributions to the Enlightenment in Paris. During assemblies and banquets of the Nine Sisters, members behaved as Masonic enlighteners; they performed scientific experiments, suggested state reform proposals, read poems and eulogies, and saw new works of art and sculpture. Yet, the most significant organizational function of the Nine Sisters revolved around the lodge's sponsorship of surrogate institutions; the lodge succeeded in promoting educational institutions and in supporting groups which favored the cause of the American Revolution. Failures too marked the cultural operations of the Nine Sisters. Unlike its counterpart in Vienna, the Lodge of the Nine Sisters failed to publish journals containing articles about the Enlightenment and Masonry and consequently did little to encourage its members to write as enlightened Masons.

NOTES

1. There are few primary and secondary sources regarding the formation and the operations of the Grand Lodge of France. Masonic scholars also do not agree about the origins and activities of this grand lodge. See Pierre Chevallier, *Histoire de la Franc-Maçonnerie Française: La Maçonnerie: École de L'Egalité,* 1725–1799 (Paris: Fayard, 1974), pp. 3–7; W. E. Moss, "Freemasonry in France in 1725–1735," *AQC*, XLVII (1934), 87–114; J. G. Findel, *History of Freemasonry*, trans. Murray Lyon (London: Asher, 1869), pp. 200–203, and Henry W. Coil, *Freemasonry Through Six Centuries* (Fulton: Ovid Bell Press, 1966), I, 230–234.

2. Findel, *History*, p. 201; and Chevallier, *Histoire de la Franc-Maçonnerie Française*, pp. 40–41.

3. Gaston Martin, *La Franc-Maçonnerie Française et La Préparation de la Revolution* (Paris, 1926), pp. 14–17.

4. Harold T. Parker, *The Cult of Antiquity*, pp. 1–2. Parker does not mention, however, the role of Freemasonry in circulating the ideas of the ancients in eighteenth century France.

5. Oliver Street, *Symbolism of the Three Degrees* (Washington: Masonic Service Association, 1922) pp. 56–57 and pp. 121–122.

6. René Le Forestier, *La Franc-Maçonnerie Templière et Occultiste aux* XVIIIe *et* XIXe Siècles (Paris: Aubier-Montaigne, 1970), pp. 29–31; and D. Ligou, "Structures et Symbolisme Maçonniques," *Annales Historiques de la Révolution Française*, CXVII (July, 1969), pp. 520–521.

7. Street, *Symbolism,* pp. 106–107 and pp. 118–121; and Albert Mackey, *Symbolism of Freemasonry* (Chicago: Powner Press, 1975), pp. 222–223.

8. Ligou, "Structures et Symbolisme Maçonniques," 521–523. Bernard Fay and other advocates of the conspiracy theory believe that by espousing the doctrines of natural liberties, French Freemasons were major contributors to the French Revolution. In *Revolution and Freemasonry* (Boston: Little Brown and Company, 1935), Bernard Fay claims that "18th Century Freemasonry fostered the revolutionary spirit" and that "the revolutionary spirit brought about the American and French Revolutions." See p. 305 and p. 314.

9. Pierre Chevallier, *Les Ducs Sous L'Acacia* (Paris: Vrin, 1964), p. 54.

10. Chevallier, *Les Ducs*, p. 55.

11. Ibid., pp. 56–57.

12. Ibid., p. 60.

13. Robert Shackleton, *Montesquieu* (London: Oxford University Press, 1961), p. 140.

14. Ibid., pp. 264–281.

15. Ibid., pp. 298–301.

16. Shackleton, *Montesquieu*, pp. 39–45; and Pauline Kra, "Religion in Montesquieu's *Lettres persanes,*" *Studies on Voltaire and the Eighteenth Century*, LXXII (1970), 35, 56–57, 90, and 110.

17. Chevallier, *Les Ducs*, p. 63. Despite being inactive in the affairs of the order, Montesquieu maintained his membership in Masonry.

18. Ibid., p. 69.

19. Ibid., p. 65 and p. 69.

20. Ibid., pp. 73–74.

21. Ibid., pp. 72–73.

22. Ibid., p. 74.

23. Ibid., pp. 76–78.

24. Chevallier, *Les Ducs*, pp. 17–18; and J. M. Roberts, *The Mythology of the Secret Societies* (London: Secker and Warburg, 1972), pp. 32–33.

25. Chevallier, *Les Ducs*, p. 183. Chevallier also claims that the *Bussi-Aumont* Lodge, which did not maintain close relations with the two other Parisian lodges, was not involved in the Jacobite controversy.

26. Chevallier, *Histoire de la Franc-Maçonnerie Française*, pp. 14–15.

27. Chevallier, *Les Ducs*, p. 101, p. 104 and p. 113.

28. However, Louis did not affiliate with Masonry.

29. Findel, *History*, p. 203; and Eugen Lennhoff, *The Freemasons*, trans. Einar Frame (London: Lewis, 1978), pp. 283–286.

30. C. N. Batham, "Chevalier Michael Ramsay: A New Appreciation" *AQC*, LXXXI (1968), 280–291; Coil, *Freemasonry Through Six Centuries*, I, 234–235; and Roberts, *Mythology*, p. 35.

31. Findel, *History*, p. 203. For alleged connections between French Freemasonry and Jacobitism, see Paul K. Monod, *Jacobitism and the English People, 1688–1788* (Cambridge: Cambridge University Press, 1989), pp. 302–304.

32. Chevallier, *Les Ducs*, pp. 143–144 and p. 149.

33. Chevallier, *Histoire de la Franc-Maçonnerie Française*, pp. 19–24; and Coil, *Freemasonry through Six Centuries*, I, 237.

34. Le Forestier, *Franc-Maçonnerie Templière*, p. 5; and Roberts, *Mythology*, p. 96. Several early leaders of the Scottish Rite might have come from Scotland, but even this point has never been substantiated. Moreover, Scottish ideas and traditions have nothing to do with Scottish Rite Masonry. Why this new Masonic system was called the Scottish rather than the French Rite has never been explained.

35. Le Forestier, *Franc-Maçonnerie Templière*, pp. 64–65; and Chevallier, *Histoire de la Franc-Maçonnerie Française*, pp. 81–82.

36. Chevallier, *Histoire de la Franc-Maçonnerie Française*, pp. 111–114.

37. Alain Bernheim, "Règlements Généraux de 1743 et Statuts de 1755," *AHRF*, CXCVII (1969), 379–384.

38. Bernheim, "Règlements Généraux." 387–390; and Alain Le Bihan, *Franc-Maçons et Ateliers Parisiens de la Grande Loge de France au XVIIIe Siècle (1760–1795)* (Paris, 1973), pp. 393–401.

39. Le Bihan, *Franc-Maçons et Ateliers Parisiens*, pp. 402–406 and pp. 429–434.

40. Ibid., pp. 481–485.

41. Ibid., pp. 473–477.

42. Albert Pike, *Morals and Dogma*, (Charleston, 1871), pp. 106–113.

43. Pike, *Morals and Dogma*, pp. 114–118: and Bernard Groethuysen, *The Bourgeois: Catholicism vs. Capitalism in Eighteenth Century France*, trans. Mary Ilford (New York: Holt, 1968), pp. 39–45.

44. Pike, *Morals and Dogma*, pp. 219–239.

45. Ibid., pp. 248–264.

46. Ibid., pp. 241–245.

47. Ibid., pp. 276–311.

48. J. Servier, "Utopie et Franc-Maçonnerie au XVIIIe Siècle," *AHRF*, CXCVII (1969), 409–413.

49. Chevallier, *Histoire de la Franc-Maçonnerie Française*, pp. 151–155; Findel, *History*, pp. 218–219; and Le Bihan, *Franc-Maçons et Ateliers Parisiens*, pp. 74–79.

50. Chevallier, *Histoire de la Franc-Maçonnerie Française,* pp. 172–177; and Martin, *Franc-Maçonnerie Française*, pp. 17–28.

51. Claude Helvétius was a major contributor to the French Enlightenment. In his major work *De l'esprit*, published in 1758, Helvétius endorses the sensationalistic concepts of Locke, maintaining that sense perceptions enabled humans to acquire knowledge and to understand the laws of Nature. In this work, he also claims that public education was essential for the amelioration of French society. Although not a contributor to the *Encyclopédie*, Helvétius participated in the circle of Diderot and d'Holbach, thus being provided with the opportunity to interact with many Parisian *philosophes*. Helvétius too was quite active in Masonry and perceived the Craft as a significant vehicle of the Enlightenment. He established in 1766 the Parisian Lodge of Science and served as Master of this lodge until his death in 1771. On his philosophical ideas and educational views, see Albert Keim, *Helvétius: Sa Vie et Son Oeuvre* (Geneva, 1970), pp. 42–46; Irving Horowitz, *Claude Helvé-*

tius: Philosopher of Democracy and Enlightenment (New York: Paine-Whitman, 1954), pp. 12–17; and D. W. Smith, *Helvétius: A Study in Persecution* (Oxford: Clarendon Press, 1965) pp. 11–13. On the involvement of Helvétius in the cultural group of d'Holbach, consult Alan Charles Kors, *D'Holbach's Coterie: An Enlightenment in Paris* (Princeton: Princeton University Press, 1976), p. 31 and p. 90. A short but important account of the role of Helvétius in Parisian Masonry is presented by Louis Amiable, *Une Loge Maçonnique D'Avant 1789* (Paris:Alcan, 1897), p. 10.

52. Amiable, *Loge Maçonnique*, pp. 14–15.

53. Ibid., p. 16.

54. Ibid., p. 18.

55. Chevallier, *Histoire de la Franc-Maçonnerie Française*, p. 280. Chevallier claims that the opponents of Lalande, for the most part, objected to the proposed name of the lodge.

56. Amiable, *Loge Maçonnique*, pp. 19–20.

57. Ibid., p. 32.

58. Ibid., p. 31.

59. Ibid., pp. 31–32.

60. Ibid., p. 30.

61. Ibid., pp. 33–34.

62. Ibid., p. 35. Amiable has included in his work the 1778 lodge roster. Franklin sent to the American Philosophical Society a listing of members from a meeting in 1780.

63. Ibid., p. 28.

64. Ibid., pp. 22–23.

65. Ibid., p. 22 and p. 26.

66. Ibid., pp. 26–28.

67. Ibid., p. 23; and Durand Echeverria, *Mirage in the West: A History of the French Image of America to 1815* (Princeton: Princeton University Press, 1957), p. 59.

68. Amiable, *Loge Maçonnique,* pp. 45–63. Amiable wrote a confusing account to explain why Voltaire made the decision to apply to the Nine Sisters. He even failed to mention Parisian Masons of the Nine Sisters who knew Voltaire.

69. Paul Hazard, *European Thought in the Eighteenth Century* (Cleveland: Meridian Books, 1963), p. 271.

70. Amiable, *Loge Maçonnique*, pp. 53–54.

71. Ibid., pp. 65–66.

72. Ibid., p. 69.

73. Ibid., pp. 68–69.

74. Ibid., pp. 82–89.

75. Ibid., p. 132.

76. Constance Salm-Salm-Dyck, *Éloge Historique de Monsieur Lalande* (Paris: Sajou, 1810), pp. 16–22; and Helene Monod-Cassidy, "Un astronome-philosophe Jerome Lalande," *Studies on Voltaire and the Eighteenth Century,* LVI (1967), 907–914.

77. Amiable, *Loge Maçonnique*, p. 133.

78. Ibid., p. 121 and p. 134.

79. Ibid., p. 134.

80. Paul W. Conner, *Poor Richard's Politicks* (New York: Oxford University Press, 1965), p. 174 and pp. 205–206; and Carl Van Doren, *Benjamin Franklin* (New York: Viking Press, 1964), pp. 156–162 and pp. 423–428.

81. Amiable, *Loge Maçonnique*, p. 137; and Esmond Wright, *Franklin of Philadelphia* (Cambridge: Belknap Press, 1986), pp. 321–322.

82. Amiable, *Loge Maçonnique*, pp. 143–144. Amiable and other historians have devoted minimal attention to the participation of Franklin in the Salon of Madame Helvétius.

83. Ibid., pp. 148–149.

84. Ibid., pp. 146–147.

85. Ibid., p. 24.

86. Echeverria, *Mirage*, p. 73.

87. Bernard Fay, *The Revolutionary Spirit in France and America*, trans. Ramon Guthrie (New York: Cooper Square Publications, 1966), p. 159.

88. Hilliard d'Auberteuil, *Essais historiques et politiques sur les Anglo-Americains* (Brussels, 1781), xiii-xiv and pp. 2–5.

89. Ibid., pp. 150–155.

90. Amiable, *Loge Maçonnique*, pp. 150–151.

91. Ibid., p. 152.

92. Amiable, *Loge Maçonnique*, p. 172; and Echeverria, *Mirage*, p. 171.

93. Amiable, *Loge Maçonnique*, pp. 172–173 and p. 175.

94. Ibid., pp. 159–176. Amiable describes the reform views of Dupaty and Pastoret, but mentions nothing about the cultural operations of the lodge during their Masterships.

95. Fay, *Revolutionary Spirit*, pp. 89–91; and Echeverria, *Mirage*, pp. 55–56.

96. Fay, *Revolutionary Spirit*, pp. 240–241; and Echeverria, *Mirage*, p. 133.

97. Amiable, *Loge Maçonnique*, p. 152 and pp. 189–190. Amiable explains that the journal of the Apollonian Society has never been found.

98. Ibid., pp. 191–193.

99. W. A. Smeaton, *Fourcroy: Chemist and Revolutionary* (Cambridge: Heffer, 1962), pp. 15–16.

100. Pilâtre de Rozier, *Premier Musée* (Paris, 1782), pp. 1–4.

101. Amiable, *Loge Maçonnique*, pp. 201–203. Amiable maintains that while teaching in the *Lycée*, Condorcet, Marmontel, and La Harpe did not belong to the Nine Sisters.

102. Robert E. Schofield, *Mechanism and Materialism: British Natural Philosophy in an Age of Reason* (Princeton: Princeton University Press, 1970), p. 235.

103. Amiable, *Loge Maçonnique*, pp. 288–289; and Richard Herr, *The Eighteenth Century Revolution in Spain* (Princeton: Princeton University Press, 1969), pp. 228–229. The Spanish diplomat Count Pena Florida was not an active participant in the Nine Sisters, but attempted to recruit several members of the lodge to the faculty of the University of Madrid. Herr maintains that Pena Florida wanted enlighteners to become members of an international fraternity devoted to the welfare of humanity.

104. Edwin Smith, *Jean Sylvain Bailly: Astronomer, Mystic, Revolutionary* (Philadelphia: American Philosophical Society, 1954), pp. 454–455.

105. Smith, *Bailly*, pp. 429–432.

106. Ibid., pp. 436–437.

107. Ibid., p. 457.

108. Ibid., pp. 466–467.

109. Richard H. Shryock, *The Development of Modern Medicine: An Interpretation of the Social and Scientific Factors Involved* (New York: Hafner, 1969), pp. 152–157.

110. Amiable, *Loge Maçonnique*, p. 282.

111. Ibid., pp. 282–283.

112. Claude Lehec and Jean Cazeneuve (eds.), *Oeuvres Philosophiques de Cabanis* (Paris, 1956), I, 6–9; and Amiable, *Loge Maçonnique*, p. 291.

113.Lehec and Cazeneuve (eds.) *Oeuvres*, I, 137–138.

114.P. J. G. Cabanis, *Sketch of the Revolutions of Medical Science*, trans. A. Henderson (London: Johnson, 1806), pp. 4–6.

115.Cabanis, *Sketch of Revolutions*, pp. 10–12.

116.Ibid., pp. 297–299 and pp. 302–305. An explanation of the role of Cabanis in the Lodge of the Nine Sisters is offered by Martin S. Staum, *Cabanis: Enlightenment and Medical Philosophy in the French Revolution* (Princeton: Princeton University Press, 1980), pp. 18–19.

117.Smeaton, *Fourcroy*, pp. 191–192.

118.Ibid., pp. 25–26 and pp. 94–95.

119.Ibid., pp. 125–126.

120.Ibid., p. 36.

121.Amiable, *Loge Maçonnique*, p. 295.

122.Claude Berthollet, *Essay on the New Method of Bleaching* (Edinburgh: Creech, 1790), pp. 21–23

123.John Forster, *An Easy Method of Assaying and Classing Mineral Substances* (London: Dilly, 1772), pp. 2–6.

124.Amiable, *Loge Maçonnique*, p. 295. For a fine explanation of the flights of the Montgolfiers, see Charles C. Gillispie, *The Montgolfier Brothers and the Invention of Aviation, 1783–1784* (Princeton: Princeton University Press, 1983), pp. 3–7, pp. 10–17, pp. 21–24, pp. 44–47, and pp. 118–120.

125.Ibid., pp. 92–93.

126.Ibid., pp. 329–331.

127.Anita Brookner, *Greuze* (Greenwich: New York Graphic Society, 1972), pp. 51–63.

128.Brookner, *Greuze*, p. 64.

129.Ibid., p. 80.

130.Levey, *Rococo to Revolution*, pp. 149–151.

131.Amiable, *Loge Maçonnique*, pp. 333–334.

132.Ibid., pp. 346–350.

133.Ibid., p. 344.

134.Ibid., p. 316 and pp. 326–327.

135.Ibid., p. 309.

136.Ibid., p. 310.

137.Louis Amiable, "Un Poeme Revolutionnaire en 1779: 'Les Mois' de Roucher," *La Révolution française*, XXIX (1895), 246.

138.Amiable, *Loge Maçonnique*, p. 316.

139.Ibid., p. 303.

140.Ibid., p. 304.

141.Jean Gaulmier, *Volney* (Paris: Hachette, 1959), pp. 21–23; and C. F. Volney, *The Ruins*. trans. Peter Eckler (New York: Truth Seeker, 1913), pp. 110–118 and pp. 184–202.

142.Court de Gébelin, *Histoire Naturelle De La Parole* (Paris: Boudet, 1776), p. 2.

143.Gébelin, *Parole*, pp. 15–18.

144.Ibid., pp. 19–23.

145.Count de Gébelin, *Monde Primitif* (Paris: Boudet, 1773), I, i.

146.Gébelin, *Monde Primitif*, I, ii-iii.

147.Ibid., I, 307–308.

148.Ibid., I, 306.

149.Ibid., I, 319–324.

150.Frank Manuel, *The Eighteenth Century Confronts the Gods*, pp. 250–254; and Count Albon, *Éloge de Court de Gébelin* (Paris: Moutard, 1785), pp. 4–9.

151.Echeverria, *Mirage*, pp. 106–108.

152.Abbé Robin, *Nouveau voyage dans l'Amérique Septentrionale* (Paris: 1782), pp. 13–17.

153.Echeverria, *Mirage*, pp. 114–115.

154.J. P. Brissot, *Nouveau voyage* (Paris, 1788), pp. 312–313.

155.Amiable, *Loge Maçonnique*, pp. 310–311; and Echeverria, *Mirage*, p. 123.

156.Amiable, *Loge Maçonnique*, p. 311.

157.Echeverria, *Mirage*, pp. 19–20. For the views of members of the Nine Sisters about America, see R. William Weisberger, "Benjamin Franklin: A Masonic Enlightener in Paris," *Pennsylvania History*, LIII (1986), pp. 165–180.

158.Amiable, *Loge Maçonnique*, pp. 300–301; and Henry Majewski, *the Preromantic Imagination of L. S. Mercier* (New York: Humanities Press, 1971), pp. 10–17.

159.Amiable, *Loge Maçonnique*, pp. 206–207.

160.Gay, *Enlightenment: Freedom*, II, 438–443.

161.Amiable, *Loge Maçonnique*, pp. 214–222.

162.Ibid., pp. 177–179.

163.Claude Pastoret, *Des Loix Pénales* (Paris, 1790), I, 1–4 and 21–23.

164.Pastoret, *Loix*, I, 60–63.

165.Ibid., I, 38–43.

166.Amiable, *Loge Maçonnique*, p. 181.

167. Some members of the Nine Sisters espoused moderate republican ideas, supported the Girondin, and participated in the affairs of the National Assembly.

168. Amiable, *Loge Maçonnique*, pp. 179–180.

169. Ibid., pp. 182–184. The Lodge of the Nine Sisters was reestablished in 1805, but its cultural operations were of minimal importance. Connections between Freemasonry and the French Revolution are explored by Lynn Hunt, *Politics, Culture, and Class in the French Revolution* (Berkeley: University of California Press, 1984), pp. 199–203; and by Gary Kates, *The Cercle Social, the Girondins, and the French Revolution* (Princeton: Princeton University Press, 1985), pp. 89–92.

170. The copyright of this essay belongs to its author. This essay has been published in the following works: R. William Weisberger, *Speculative Freemasonry and the Enlightenment: A Study of the Craft in London, Paris, Prague, and Vienna* (New York: East European Monograph Series of Columbia University Press, 1993), pp. 65–107; R. William Weisberger, Wallace McLeod, and S. Brent Morris (eds.), *Freemasonry on Both Sides of the Atlantic: Essays Concerning the Craft in the British Isles, the United States, and Mexico* (New York: East European Monograph Series of Columbia University Press, 2002), pp. 299–345; and *Heredom*, X (2002), 155–202.

A BRIEF REVIEW OF ANTI MASONRY ... 1698 TO 2005

◆

BY YASHA BERESINER, LL.B

Introduction

350 years is a hefty chunk of History. There have been many changes since Elias Ashmole was initiated into freemasonry—as we understand that term today—on the 16 of October 1646 in Warrington. Technology has surpassed levels of our imagination and the success of the freemasonry we practice today must be well beyond the greatest hopes and expectations of our founding forefathers.

One thing, however, has not changed, human nature. Envy, jealousy, spite, greed and ambition among men was there long before 1646 and will be there long after the year 2000. And so far as anti-masonry goes.... *plus ca change plus c'est la même chose!*

In 1698 a small size pamphlet was distributed in the streets of London warning Londoners *to be aware of those who call themselves Freed masons* as ... *they are evil and mischievous....* In 1991 Martin Short author of *Inside the Brotherhood,* the sequel to Stephen Knight's *The Brotherhood,* used almost identical words, calling Freemasonry an evil Institution and its members mischievous in their activities. Three hundred years and the same words are used and same sentiments are expressed. You see what I mean when I say *plus ca change plus c'est la même chose!*

The pamphlet I mentioned—the earliest overt evidence we have of antagonism toward our Society—is an exceedingly important document in the history of anti-masonry and needs further consideration. It consists of a single small sized leaflet, 100mm by 165mm, set in the Roman type and of which only one single original copy is extant in the Library and Museum of the United Grand Lodge of England in London. It is headed *To All Godly People, in the Citie of London* and dated at the base *1698,* nearly two decades before the formation of the premier Grand Lodge. The text reads as follows:

> *Having thought it needful to warn you/of the Mischiefs*
> *and Evils practiced/in the Sight of GOD by those called/*
> *Freed Masons, I say take Care lest their Cer-/emonies*
> *and secret Swearings take hold of/you; and be weary that*
> *none cause you to err/from Godliness. For this Devlish*
> *sect of/Men are Meeters in secret which swear against/*
> *all without their Following. They are the/Anti Christ*
> *which was to come leading/Men from Fear of GOD. For how*
> *should/Men meet in secret Places and with secret/Signs*
> *taking Care that none observe them to/do the Work of*
> *GOD; are not these the Ways/of Evil-doers?*
> *Knowing how that GOD observeth pri-/villy them that sit*
> *in Darkness they shall be/smitten and the Secrets of*
> *their Hearts layed/bare. Mingle not among this corrupt*
> *People/lest you be found so at the World's Conflag-/*
> *ration.*

In three lines outside the body of the text, at the base, it says:

> *Set forth as a Warning to this Christian Generation by/*
> *M Winter, and Printed by R Sare at Gray's/Inn-gate, in*
> *Holborn./1698.*

Very little information of the circumstances under which the pamphlet was issued are known. There is no information of M Winter, who must clearly have been the author. The time period and context within which the leaflet was issued, however, are of relevance and interest. In the leaflet freemasonry is condemned for the anti-religious standing of its membership. Knoop and Jones in their short paper published in AQC 55 (1942) give a prime example of how much important and consequential information can be obtained from the content of this simple leaflet. They were able to speculate and conclude on the possibility that Winter, the author, was pious, probably a chiliast, condemning the masons as crypto-Romanists. That these denunciations in the leaflet in 1698 may have been based on fact although there was no reason for the masons to be accused of popery. The content of the leaflet affirms that Freemasonry was considered an evil institution because of the secret signs and meeting places.

The oaths referred to in the pamphlet do not correspond to the obligations we take today, the leaflet indicates that oaths were taken against all non-masons. They were more likely to be an interpretation of operative practices. The term 'Freed' masons is a term referring to members of the London Company—the Worshipful Company of Masons of the City of London—which traces its Grant of Arms to the year 1472. What was clear is that at the time of the distribution of the leaflet, Masonic oaths and secret meeting places were considered to be anti-social.

Winter may have genuinely believed the masons to be involved in plots against the Government. The freemasons were seen as Socinians (deniers of the divinity of Christ) and the term *antichrist* is used in the leaflet to support Gnostic and Judaising controversy. The most interesting conclusion reached by Knoop and Jones is that the statement in the leaflet that the Masons were antichrist implies that they were anti-Trinitarian. Therefore freemasonry may well have adopted a deistic attitude toward religion long before Anderson's constitutions of 1723.

The implication of the very existence of this leaflet, which, incidentally was discovered by Bro Albert Frost of Sheffield and donated by him to the Grand Lodge Library in 1943, is that Freemasonry in 1698 was of sufficient consequence to justify such an attack. Had we been an organisation, one of the many hundreds of the period, of inconsequential activity, we would have been ignored. From a viewpoint of classification only, the 1698 pamphlet is seen as a religious attack on freemasonry. It was the first of a long series of such attacks.

The Papal Bulls

When considering anti-religious aspects of freemasonry, the Papal Bulls instantly come to mind. In 1738 the well-known Papal Bull *In Eminenti* was issued by Pope Clement XII. He was born as Lorenzo Corsini and became Pope in 1720. Totally incidentally, in July 1999 I had the privilege of befriending Count Giovanni Corsini in Florence, a direct descendant of Clement the XII and our fascinating exchanges on his views of his own ancestry and its connotations to freemasonry, continue to date. He is not a freemason. The 1738 Papal Bull prohibited Catholics from becoming Freemasons under the penalty of excommunication. There followed a series of Bulls and Edicts emanating from the Vatican confirming the hostility of the Catholic Church toward the Freemasons. The subject of Papal Bulls, which remains the greatest manifestation of the controversial concept of Papal infallibility, has been extensively covered in Masonic literature. They are the most overt reflection of the Church's hostility to freemasonry.

The word *Bull* is derived from the Latin *bulla* which, in Roman times, described any type of decorative stud used on armour or doors. In Etruscan times the *Bulla* was worn as a charm, often in the shape of a heart. This may be the origin of the ecclesiastic practice of attaching a metal ingot suspended by variously coloured ribbons to the end of official documents. The Papal Bull is at the top of a list in order of importance, of the communications emanating from the Vatican. Lesser matters were communicated by briefs, regulations and edicts, *inter alia*.

The Bull was initially hand written in Latin on vellum parchment in elaborate calligraphy using convoluted terminology. The folding and formal sealing of the document would involve a painstaking ceremony at the end of which the Papal seal was applied to a metal ingot, the *Bullæ*. The Papal Bull was now authenticated. The Bull, often accompanied by a translation to facilitate its understanding, was then printed in Rome and distributed to all the local dioceses. The publication entailed a formal ceremony in which the Bishop officially proclaimed the Bull, which was then read at several church services. Thereafter, the printed version was appended to the door of the Church ... until it was torn down or discarded after a suitable period of time. The evidence for this procedure can be found on many of the documents themselves.

As mentioned above, the first Papal Bull relevant to freemasonry was the well documented *In Eminenti* issued by Pope Clement XII on 28 April 1738. It was given in Rome at the Basilica of St Mary the Greater. The very last line of the printed document states:

> '... *Publicata fuit ad valvas Basilicae Principis*
> *Apostolorum ac aliis locis solitis consuetis, &c.'*

which translates as: *Published on the doors of St Peter's and other usual places.* The first English version of *In Eminenti* was published in the 1754 edition of Scott's Pocket companion. The second Bull of Benedict XIV in 1751, *Providas*, is even more detailed in the requirements of its dissemination. The last paragraph, following the signature and seal, freely translated, states *inter alia*:

> ... *the above mentioned Constitution was affixed and*
> *published on the doors of the Lateran Basilica and of the*
> *Chief of the Apostles, etc etc; and in other customary*
> *and usual places by me, Franciscus Bartolotti, Apost.*
> *Pursuivant.*

The legality of this mode of publication, by posting the printed document onto church doors and 'other usual places', is further stressed in contemporary ephemeral documents issued by various civic authorities. An example is the Italian Proclamation in Rome dated 14 January 1739, repeating the Vatican's prohibitions on freemasonry and ending with the statement:

> '... the present proclamation, when affixed in the usual
> places in Rome, do oblige and bind Rome and its
> District ... in the same manner as if they had been
> personally notified to each of them....'

The considerable and dramatic changes in world affairs, between the publication of *Providas* in 1751 and the next Papal Bull of relevance to freemasonry in 1821, appears to have made no difference at all to the Vatican. The contrary seems to be the case. Freemasonry and the *Carbonari* are now identified with each other in the two Bulls by Pope Pius VII, *Ecclesiam a Jesu Christo* in 1821 and *Quo Graviora* 1825. The latter incorporates and quotes in full all three previous Papal Bulls condemning freemasonry. As to the authority by which it is published, its legality and distribution, Section 20 of the document, the penultimate paragraph, states:

> '... exactly the same credit will be given to printed
> copies of these our Letters subscribed by the hand of
> some Public Notary, and fortified by the seal of someone
> invested with ecclesiastical dignity, as would be given
> to the very original letter exhibited or produced.'

This was the method of communicating officially and with authority, the word of the Holy See to the faithful across the nation. The most expressive manifestation of the importance and power of the Papal Bulls is the existence of exceedingly rare examples of forgeries. They were issued in printed form only to support and enforce illegal, or at least unofficial, rules and regulations applied by some authorities or other. They are considered priceless documents today often exceeding the religious-historic value of the original documents. The hostility of the Vatican toward freemasonry, however, should be placed within its true context. It would be misleading to suggest that the Papal Bulls were, from the beginning, directed at Freemasonry worldwide. The implications appear to be the fear of the Vatican early in the 18th Century, at a time when secular and religious power lay with the Pope, at the appearance in Italy, in Florence specifically, of

Masonic Lodges and their implied secrecies. This is further confirmed by the later Papal Bulls which make specific reference to the *Carbonari,* with whom Freemasonry was indiscriminately, and quite erroneously, identified.

There were practical repercussions to the Papal Bulls. In Italy, Tommaso Crudeli, the famous jurist, poet and teacher had been initiated into the first English Lodge in Florence in 1735. In May 1739 he was arrested by the Inquisition for nothing more than his involvement with Freemasonry. His involvement with the English Lodge is reflected in the minutes of the Grand Lodge of England where it is recorded that £ 20.00 was voted, in 1739, for the relief of Crudeli, then imprisoned. He remained in prison for 16 months and was later under house arrest where many of his poems were written, describing the tortuous circumstances of his unjust imprisonment.

In 1738 a royal edict supporting the Papal Bull was issued in Portugal banning Freemasonry and the case of John Coustos, a British subject and another victim of the Inquisition, is a well known incident of the period. He was initiated in London and continued his Masonic activities in Paris—where a Lodge is today named after him—before settling in Lisbon in 1742. Not withstanding the ban on Freemasonry, he was the founding member and first Master of a Lodge in the City. Due to some internal friction, the activities of the Lodge were reported to the Portuguese Inquisition and Coustos with some other Brethren were arrested in that same year. Although sentenced to imprisonment for four years, and supposedly tortured to reveal the secrets of Freemasonry, he was soon released due to the intervention of the Duke of Newcastle, then the Secretary of State. On his return to England, Coustos published his book *The Sufferings of John Coustos,* which saw the light of day in 1746, the year of his death.

Incidentally, John Coustos' version of events and claims in his book of having suffered heavy torture (even illustrating some of the torture instruments used) were repudiated when the official documents of the records of the Inquisition were released. Details of these documents have been published in Volumes 81 and 92 of AQC, the Transactions of the Quatuor Coronati Lodge. John Coustos' book has allowed the modern Historian to have an important insight into the activities of expatriate Freemasons during this early period of Freemasonry in Europe.

As a footnote it is interesting to note that when the present Archbishop of Canterbury was appointed in January 2003, there was considerable press coverage about his antagonism to Freemasonry. In correspondence that followed with the United Grand Lodge of England, the Archbishop informed Grand Lodge that his views had been misrepresented, his father had been a member of the Craft and that he, the Archbishop, had only respect for the Craft and its activities.

Masonic Exposures

Many early publications of this kind have been an important source of reference to the modern student. None, however, are as useful as the series of works known as exposures. An exposure may be defined as a publication—normally in the form of a catechism—disclosing the supposed secrets of the Freemasons.

Let us accept the maxim that for all practical purposes there are only two secrets in Freemasonry: the words and the signs of recognition leading from one degree to the next. It will be appreciated, therefore, that the spelling in full of such words or the illustration or description of the signs, may be seen as a breach of our secrets and thus be considered an attack on the Craft.

In this context the earliest exposure detailing our ceremony of initiation was published in a London newspaper, *the Flying Post* in April of 1723. It was intended to coincide with the publication of James Anderson's first *Book of Constitutions* and did so within weeks. A number of additional exposures appeared and the most important of these by far was Samuel Prichard's *Masonry Dissected* published in October 1730. There is no doubt or argument on the intent of the author and publisher in having the booklet printed: monetary gain and the satisfaction of the curiosity of the general public.

But could there be such outstanding curiosity on the part of the general public to justify three editions of *Masonry Dissected* within just eleven days? Advertisements in the local press offering *Masonry Dissected* for sale show a new second edition published the day after the first and a third edition ten days later. At the time of this publication London was saturated with societies and fraternities of every kind, of which freemasonry was only one. The majority of the population who would have been interested in the activities of such societies were still illiterate. The only conclusion, therefore, as to great popularity of *Masonry Dissected* at the time of its publication is that freemasons themselves were buying the pamphlet as an *aide memoir*.

The great importance of *Masonry Dissected* lies in that here for the very first time we see the Hiramic Legend as a separate third degree and as practised today. A publication detailing the ritual working following on the very recent introduction of the degree must have come as a blessing to many of the Brethren eager to learn and practice this new aspect of freemasonry.

The Premier Grand Lodge, under pressure at this time with Freemasonry on the decline, became concerned with the publication of *Masonry Dissected* particularly the danger now that non-masons gaining access to Lodges may also benefit from charitable aspects of the fraternity. In their misguided wisdom, Grand Lodge decided as a preventive measure to change the first and second degree words and signs in an effort to detect impostors. This action by Grand Lodge was to have major consequences. *Masonry Dissected* was such a successful publication that no other exposures were published in England until 1760.

By now a new and competing Grand Lodge had been formed. In 1751 a number of Brethren of Irish descent formed themselves into a Grand Lodge claiming, as an excuse, the deviation of the Premier Grand Lodge from the landmarks of the order. These landmarks included the transposition of the first and second degree words and signs, as already described above as well as various other factors, such as the non-recognition of the Royal Arch as part of ancient Freemasonry. The new Grand Lodge, which soon became known as the ANTIENTS, was almost immediately under the effective control of a most formidable Freemason, Laurence Dermott who became its Grand Secretary within a year of its foundation. They successfully dubbed the earlier Premier Grand Lodge of 1717 as the Moderns and the term has remained in use to date. Although independent, quite clearly the new Grand Lodge was strongly influenced in all its aspects by the Grand Lodge of Ireland. This was also manifest in its ritual workings. From the start there was great animosity between the two Grand Lodges, which effectively continued till the Union of 1813.

Now that two different and competing Grand Lodges existed in England was an opportunity for anonymous authors to publish new exposures detailing the different working of the two Grand Lodges. In 1760 we have the first edition *of Three Distinct Knocks.* The introduction states that the content is the working of the three degrees of the Antients Grand Lodge. Two years later in 1762, *Jachin and Boaz* was published, relating to the working of the Moderns (claiming, no doubt in an attempt to increase sales, that the ritual described applied to both Grand Lodges). Both these books went into many editions, as did, indeed, did Samuel Prichard's *Masonry Dissected.*

The final reconciliation between the two Grand Lodges, which led to the formation of the United Grand Lodge of England in December of 1813, did not put a stop to further publications of Masonic exposures. The differences between the two Grand Lodges were not easily reconciled. Not least was the problem arising from the fact that the older Premier Grand Lodge, the Moderns, advocated the practice of three and only three degrees under its jurisdiction. The Antients, on the other hand, permitted Lodges to practice any of the additional orders beyond the craft under the authority of their Craft warrant. This was a major point of contention and a problem that the Duke of Sussex, the new Grand Master of the United Grand Lodge of England, had to resolve at the time of the Union in 1813. The problems were resolved in a Solomonic fashion by the second Article of the Constitutions of the United Grand Lodge of England, which stated that:

> *Pure Ancient Masonry consists of three degrees and no more, namely those of the EA, the FC and the MM including the Supreme Order of the Royal Arch.*

This disposed of the Royal Arch, undoubtedly a most important aspect and the major point of contention between the Antients and the Moderns. The matter of the remaining orders, of which a great number were now flourishing among a large number of Brethren, were dealt with by the additional statement in the Article:

> *But this article is not intended to prevent any Lodge or Chapter from holding a Meeting in any of the degrees of the Orders of Chivalry, according to the constitutions of the said Orders.*

This was a compromise the Duke of Sussex was not happy with. He had too much on his plate in his efforts to secure a successful Union to have to worry and bother with a handful of additional Orders. His attitude was to ignore and effectively suppress all additional Orders. The Union was considered to be a tragedy to the adherents of the many smaller Orders. A number continued to practice and attend meetings but the overall picture is one of diminishing activity and popularity.

And yet, in 1826 we have the publication in England of a new exposure titled *The Ritual of Freemasonry* by an established and well known spokesman for the freedom of speech. Richard Carlisle was in prison when he began his attack on the Freemasons by publishing aspects of the ritual in his newspaper *The Republican*. The articles were incorporated into his book detailing now the ritual working of all the available degrees and Orders beyond the Craft. What a blessing to the dwindling number of Masons who are now able to keep alive their Orders until better times. It is somewhat ironic that a publication intended as a major attack on the freemasons should prove to be the cause of the survival of the many additional orders. These came to their own with the passing of the Duke of Sussex in 1843, while still active as Grand Master, and now replaced by more liberal 2nd Earl of Zetland.

William Morgan and Politics

There are and have been throughout history, political movements that have made a point of targeting Freemasonry. These began, as stated earlier, with the Church in the 18th Century when much secular power lay in its hands and the State was influenced by the Church. It has continued in a long line of repression of Freemasonry by many Governments—not least in the Middle East and, until recently, in most of the Eastern Europe countries. A number of politicians and Governments may have some historical justification for their concerns. We may consider that the South American sub continent was liberated from the Spanish yoke by Freemasons. All the South American heroes of the early 19th century were freemasons and many Lodges today bear their names: Simón Bolívar, Antonio José de Sucre, Ambrose Higgins and José de San Martín, amongst them.

The most overt example, however, of the influence of politics on Freemasonry remains the extra-ordinary case in America, the mother of democracy and liberty. It is the famous case known as the William Morgan affair, which took place in 1826, when the whole nation, through its political arm, turned violently against the Craft. Freemasonry suffered for the best part of a quarter century and was only back on the road to recovery in the 1860s. The case remains extraordinary for several reasons. The whereabouts of Morgan himself are still a mystery and the near hysterical over-reaction of the populace, on what was in effect a minor incident, has still to be explained.

William Morgan, for reasons that are not apparent, was refused entry to a lodge in Batavia, New York and decided to take his revenge by colluding with the editor of the *Republican Advocate,* one David Miller, to disclose the secrets of Freemasonry in a book. Shortly after this collusion became known, in September 1826, Morgan disappeared and the Freemasons were effectively accused of his murder. A political party relying entirely on an Anti-Masonic ticket was formed relying totally on the theory that Morgan was abducted by force by the Freemasons and was violently assassinated. The attacks on Freemasonry that followed are without precedence. The facts and statistics show a devastating picture:

- In 1828 a mason and an anti mason ran for Governor of New York; the former, Martin van Buren had some 136,000 votes in his favour whilst the anti-mason, Solomon Southwick received only 33,000 votes. Just 2 years later in the same elections the anti Masonic candidate won 120,000 votes against only 128,000 for the winning candidate!

* By 1832 there were a total of 141 Anti Masonic newspapers published throughout the United States.

* In 1826 the Grand Lodge of New York had just over 500 Lodges under its jurisdiction. These dwindled down to only 65 in 1846.

* 20,000 freemasons in 1825 were reduced to a mere 3,000 members in 1830.

Fortunately recovery was rapid after 1862 and the statistics were healthy again with 430 lodges boasting a revived membership of some 25,000 freemasons. New York was typical of many of the other States in America. This American experience, which led to untold crisis in the personal lives of many families, has no precedence in Masonic history. It is an example of political bigotry and public enticement at its worst extreme.

Morgan's book was published as an illustrated exposure titled *Light on Masonry*. His case is still used today when Freemasonry is attacked, with little reference to the facts and figures of this black period in American Masonic History.

How much change has there been in attitudes toward freemasonry in the last hundred years? I would suggest very little indeed. England remains the mother Grand Lodge of all nations and we can look at recent events in London as a reflection of attitudes toward our Craft. It is not all good news. In February of 1997 the Home Affairs Committee of the House of Commons decided to look into the question of Freemasonry in the Police and the Judiciary. The final report was overwhelmingly favourable toward freemasonry. A long list of Judges, Magistrates and other members of the judiciary, (which included Lord Mackay, the Lord High Chancellor) and high ranking policemen were called as witnesses and unequivocally stated that they found nothing in freemasonry that adversely effected the Judiciary or the Police. The one exception was the Chief Police Officer who felt that *membership* (by policemen) *of organisations such as Freemasonry was undesirable.* Paragraph 32 of the report stated:

Para. 32: *The Committee conclude that, when the oath are read in context, there is nothing in them that would appear sinister, and nothing in the evidence that we have heard that would show a conflict between the oath taken by a judge or policeman and that by a freemason.*

We do not believe that there is anything sinister about freemasonry, properly observed, and are confident that freemasonry itself does not encourage malpractice.

Notwithstanding the positive aspects of the report, the enquiry recommended that a register should be made available to the public of all those involved in the administration of criminal justice and freemasons should be identified on the register! The final and concluding report of the Committee reads as follows:

> Para 56: *It is obvious that there is a great deal of unjustified paranoia about free-masonry and we have no wish to add to it. We believe that there would be practi-cal difficulties in requiring a register of freemasons in all areas of the Criminal Justice system, but it would certainly be possible to establish one. We also note that the Prime Minister himself has said that he was in favour of a requirement for public officials to declare whether they are freemasons or not, and that the Shadow Home Secretary believes that membership of the freemasons should be a declarable and registered interest. We believe however that nothing so much undermines pub-lic confidence in public institutions as the knowledge that some public servants are members of a secret society one of whose aims is mutual self-advancement—or a column of mutual support to use the Masonic phrase. We note the claim by United Grand Lodge that freemasons are not a secret society but a society with secrets. We believe, however, that this distinction is lost on most non-masons. The solution is not bans or proscriptions or any form of intolerance. We acknowledge that a lot of honest people derive innocent social pleasure from membership of freemasonry and we have no wish to deprive them of such pleasure. The solution is disclosure. We recommend that police officers, magistrates, judges and crown prosecutors should be required to register membership of any secret society and that the record should be available publicly. However, it is our firm belief that the better solution lies in the hands of freemasonry itself. By openness and disclosure, all suspicion would be removed and we would welcome the taking of such steps by the United Grand Lodge.*

The United Grand Lodge of England issued a seven point News Release on 25 March 1997 signed by the Grand Secretary repudiating this final conclusion of the Committee as set out in Paragraph 56 of the report. There was no further action taken on the matter until after the election of May 1997 when the new Labour Government came into power and pursued the matter further.

A new Home Affairs Committee, under the Chairmanship of Christopher Mullin MP, was appointed in February 1998 and consisted entirely of new mem-bers, who had not been involved in the Committee a year earlier, with the sole exception of the Chairman himself. This time there were specific allegations of a Masonic conspiracy involving police corruption. The United Grand Lodge of

England was represented at the open and fully televised sessions by the then Grand Secretary, Commander Michael Higham (who retired in May 1998) and by John Hamill, Head of Communications at Grand Lodge. The Committee produced three lists containing 199 names and Grand Lodge was required to identify those on the lists who were Freemasons. The initial refusal of the Grand Secretary to disclose such information in the absence of any specific allegations against the named individuals was to no avail. At the end, only 17 of the 199 names proved to be members of the Craft. These were handed to the Committee under protest. The Home Affairs Committee did not pursue the matter further. The United Grand Lodge of England issued the following communication on 25 May 1999:

Home Affairs Committee Clears Freemasons

Freemasons will be pleased, but not surprised, that the Home Affairs Select Committee has reached the following conclusions:

- *"Freemasonry was not a primary cause of the difficulties within the West Midlands Serious Crime Squad"*

- *"Freemasonry was not a significant factor in the Birmingham pub bombings case"*

- *We cannot conclude Freemasonry played a significant part in the Stalker Affair"*

Despite a lengthy investigation, Mr Mullin, MP and his committee have produced no evidence that Freemasons were involved in any possible miscarriage of justice in these three high profile cases.

The committee acknowledges there is "a great deal of unjustified paranoia about Freemasonry." Freemasons heartily agree.

Today, in England, every member of the judiciary and police, if asked, is still required to sign a form indicating his membership of the Craft, if he is a freemason. It is an amazing and disconcerting political requirement. This in spite of legislation by the European Court of Human Rights in July 2001 declaring explicitly that 'Freemasonry is neither a Secret Society nor a Criminal Association' and that denying any man any right because of his being a Freemason is illegal and a breach of his human rights. As I said at the beginning, envy, spite, greed and ambition have been the determining and constant factors affecting the attitudes of those who have had malignant designs toward us through the years.

Is it a consoling thought, that only successful organisations are those that are attacked? That another more dangerous trait than hatred toward us would be indifference? It seems to me that as long as there is no indifference toward Free-masonry, we will continue and go through the coming years and centuries with the same success, the same high moral standards that have distinguished our organisation from the many other similar institutions through the past centuries.

Bibliography & Credits:

Brodsky, Michel L *The Reality of Anti-Masonry* Heredom Vol 2 Washington 1993F

Crawley, W J Chetwode, *The Old Charges and Papal Bulls* AQC 24(1911)

Hamill, John, *Contemporary anti-Masonry in England* Masonic Perspectives, The Australian Masonic Research Council, Victoria, Australia 1992

Jackson A C F *English Masonic Exposures 1760–1769* Middx 1986

Knoop, Douglas; Jones, G P & Hamer, Douglas *The Early Masonic Catechisms,* QC London 1975

Knoop, Douglas; Jones, G P & Hamer, Douglas *Early Masonic Pamphlets,* QC London 1978

McLeod, Wallace *Responding to Criticism* The Quest for Light, The Australian & New Zealand Masonic Research Council, Melbourne, Australia 1997

Read, Will *The Church of Rome and Freemasonry* AQC 104 (1991)

Robbins, Alfred F *The Earliest Years of English Organised Freemasonry* AQC 22, (1909)

Tatsch J H *American Masonic crisis, the Morgan incident of 1826* AQC 34 (1921)

United Grand Lodge News—various. Newsletters freely distributed following on the Quarterly Communications of the United Grand Lodge of England Press Information. Issued from the Office of the Director of Communications.

Vatcher Dr S *John Coustos and the Portuguese Inquisition* AQC 81 (1968)

Yasha Beresiner, LL.B. PGStB (UGLE); PSGW (RGLItaly); HonSGW (GLSIsrael). PM Quatuor Coronati Lodge No 2076 (England) The Premier Lodge of Masonic Research.

Bro Yasha Beresiner will welcome correspondence and can be contacted through his web site: www.intercol.co.uk

PASSING THE VEILS: ITS HISTORICAL DEVELOPMENT AND SYMBOLISM

✦

BY PETER J. MILLHEISER, MD, FACS

Some of the most fascinating changes that have occurred in the Royal Arch Masonry ritual have been those of the legends of the vault and the veils. Philostorgius, the great fourth century historian, wrote that as the Roman Emperor, Julian was attempting to rebuild the city of Jerusalem, a stone was dislodged revealing a hidden vault. Workers were lowered into the vault whose dimensions formed a perfect square. One of the workers struck his foot against a column upon which was found a book wrapped in a fine linen cloth. His companions outside the vault then pulled this worker up by a rope tied around his waist. The book appeared new, and written in the book in large letters was the Gospel of John, "In the beginning was the Word, and the Word was with God, and the Word was God."

There were other variations of the vault legend. In the book of *Enoch*, Enoch had a vision from God of nine vaults and he proceeded to build a secret sanctuary based on the plan that had been revealed to him. The vaults were built one under the other and in the ninth or lowest vault was a triangle of the purist gold upon which was inscribed the name of God.

The rituals of both the vault legend and the Passing of the Veils changed throughout Masonic history, being de-Christianized in both England and the United States in the 18th and early 19th centuries.

In the Bible, there are various references to the veil of the temple. In *Exodus 26:31–33*, it was written:

And thou shalt make a veil of blue and purple and scarlet and fine twined linen of cunning work: with cherubim shall it be made: And thou shalt hang it upon four pillars of shittim wood overlaid with gold ... And thou shalt hang up the veil under the taches, that thou mayest bring in thither within the veil the ark of the testimony: and the veil shall divide unto you between the holy place and the most holy.

Flavius Josephus in *the Antiquities of the Jew, (3:7:7)* described the veils of the tabernacle whose colors represented the four elements from which the earth was created:

The veils too were composed of four things, they declared the four elements; for the fine linen was proper to signify the earth, because the flax grows out of the earth; the purple signified the sea, because that color is dyed by the blood of a sea-shellfish.; the blue is fit to signify the air; and the scarlet will naturally be an indication of fire.

The symbolism of the veils was important in the New Testament. In *Matthew 27:51,* it was written: "And, behold, the veil of the temple was rent in twain from the top to the bottom: and the earth did quake, and the rocks rent ..." In *Hebrews 10:19, 20,* the veil is referred to as the flesh of Jesus. "By a new and living way, which he hath consecrated for us, through his veil which is to say his flesh ..."

In late 18th century England, Chapter minutes, as well as various manuscripts, contain records of the working of the Passing of the Veils. The Passing of the Veils was not a universal custom in the early English Chapter degrees and the ceremony fell into abeyance in the 19th century. The Passing of the Veils was most commonly practiced in England in the period when the Royal Arch was still a Trinitarian Christian degree. The degree was de-Christianized, first with the union of the Grand Chapters of the Antients and Moderns in 1813, and subsequently with a more extensive reworking of the Chapter degrees in 1834–35.

Prior to this, there was a degree called the Excellent Master Degree, in which the Passing of the Veils took place. This degree is not related to the present Most Excellent Master Degree. The Excellent Master Degree was abandoned in England when the degrees were reworked and the ceremony of the Veils in England generally fell into disuse. In the United States, the Excellent Master Degree was also dropped from the Chapter degrees in the revision of the degrees at the beginning of the formation of the General Grand Chapter in 1797. Unlike

England, the Passing of the Veils was incorporated into the Royal Arch Degree in the United States.

However, the Passing of the Veils did not fully disappear in England. Some English Chapters continued to work the ceremony as part of Royal Arch Masonry. Utilizing the minutes and the treasurer's books of some of the Yorkshire Chapters, such as the Chapter of Affability, it was found that the ceremony of the veils continued to be used until at least the 1860's.

The Passing of the Veils in England, when practiced following the reforms of 1834–35, generally occurred with the Exaltation. These two ceremonies were held on the same day and the Passing of the Veils preceded the Exaltation. However, in a number of cases, the Exaltation preceded the Passing of the Veils by as much as four years.

By the latter part of the 19th century, there is no evidence that the Veils ceremony was still being worked in England. However, in 1899, masons in Bristol, in the west of England, decided to research the Passing of the Veils and to reincorporate it into the Royal Arch Degree. There was no information about the ceremony that they could find. Ernest Henry Cook, who was the last surviving member of this group of masons, some 30 years later described how they recreated the ritual. Initially three veils were suspended in an anteroom adjoining the Chapter room. A fourth veil was subsequently added. It is unclear if the ceremony of the veils worked in the 19th century in England was the same as the pre-union workings of the 18th and very early 19th centuries.

The ceremony that we can recreate from the 19th century consisted of the Junior Scribe conducting the candidate and giving four knocks at the door of the First Veil. The High Priest read from the third chapter of *Exodus*, verses 1 to 6, concerning the Burning Bush, at which point the bandage was removed from the candidate's eyes. This was followed by the 13th and 14th verses of the same chapter. At the second veil, the readings were of the serpent and of Aaron's rod. The passwords were Moses, Aaron, and Eleazer. Within the third veil, the miracles of the leprous hand and the pouring of water on the dry land were discussed. The candidate was then shown the various holy articles and was able to present himself as a Sojourner.

The working of the Passing of the Veils is still performed in other countries. The Irish ceremony seems to be the one most closely related to the American ceremony, both of which use four veils. The veils ceremony is also worked in Scotland, and in parts of Canada and Australia. In Queensland, Australia, the signs of the veils are similar to the American signs, but the ceremony is enacted in the Excellent Master Degree which has been retained. The candidate is taught the grips, which accompany the signs of the three veils. The candidate, however, does not pass through the white veil.

In the United States, Royal Arch Masonry made an early appearance. The first recorded minutes of a Royal Arch Exaltation in the world were in the lodge in Fredericksburg, Virginia, on December 22, 1753, when Daniel Campbell, Robert Hatherston, and Alexander Wodrons were raised to the degree of Royal Arch Mason. This was the same lodge in which George Washington was initiated on November 4, 1753. A Royal Arch Chapter was also held in Philadelphia in 1758. St. Andrews Royal Arch Chapter in Massachusetts, in the 18th century, originally worked four degrees, the Excellent, Super-Excellent, Royal Arch, and Knight Templar degrees. These degrees were all given in one night.

In 1797, plans were made to form the General Grand Chapter, which then proceeded to reconcile differences, which existed in the rituals used by the various American Chapters. Under the leadership of Thomas Smith Webb, the Chapter ritual was standardized to the format of the four degrees used today.

The symbolism of the veils is complex. *Chronicles II, 3:14* describes how Solomon made the veil of the temple of fine linen in blue, purple, and crimson. The same colors used in the veils were also worked into the robes of the High Priest. The passage through the veils is a passage to the sacred place (the Holiest of Holies) to receive spiritual illumination. Passing through the veils is a symbol of the trials and difficulties that are encountered in the search for Truth. As the veils separated the Holy places from the Holiest of Holies, which was regarded as a heaven peculiar to God, so the veil screening the Holiest of Holies was also the boundary between earth and heaven.

Blue, the color of the first veil, is the symbol of friendship and benevolence, the first step in the search for Truth. As the blue of the sky represents the threshold of heaven, so the blue veil is the threshold of the mystical passageway through the veils to illumination.

Purple, the color of the second veil, is the symbol of union of the colors blue and red, and refers to the connection of Craft (blue) and Royal Arch Masonry (red). This is the color of the intermediate degrees.

The scarlet or third veil, which is symbolic of fervency and zeal, shows that the candidate has advanced and will be successful in his journey from darkness to light. Red is the basic symbol of the strength, vitality, and power of life. The name Adam in Hebrew is closely related to the Hebrew word for red and so red is symbolic of the vitality of Adam, which has continued throughout time.

White, the color of the fourth veil, is the universal symbol of purity and teaches the candidate that only by purity of life can he expect to be worthy of receiving the Divine Truth. To Plato, white was the color of the gods. At the transfiguration of Jesus on Mount Tabor, his clothes became dazzling white. The word candidate means one dressed in white and white is the color of initiation. In Hebrew, the word for white is related to the word for perfection.

Only after going through the illumination of the veils, is one entitled to receive the Signet of Truth, enabling him to pass the final veil separating the Holy from the Holiest of Holies. The Passing of the Veils symbolizes the mystical journey to illumination and enlightenment. An old Lancastershire English Craft Lecture about 1800 noted that the Veil of the Temple signified Jesus hanging upon the Alter of the cross as the true veil between God and man, shadowing man with his wounds and blood.

"Taking the Veil" has also been a symbol of separating a life with God from that of the outside world, as when a nun "takes the veil". In Islam, the veil divides the damned from the chosen. The Sufi Moslems state that a person is veiled when he cannot perceive the Divine Light in his heart. In Buddhism, there is a veil, *Maya,* which conceals the ultimate reality. The veil is also protective, as the unscreened Light of Truth could be blinding. Moses covered his face at the burning bush to shade his eyes. To the Moslems, the face of God is veiled by 70 thousand curtains of light and darkness without which everything God gazed upon would be burned up. The veil can also be seen as a method of communication as it only partially conceals, permitting some light to penetrate the veil. Another interpretation is that the veils represented the sufferings of the Jewish people in returning from Babylonian exile.

Illumination from within, based on the passing through the veils, is an alchemical interpretation. The object of the alchemical art is the uncovering of the inner faculty of wisdom, removing the veils, which separate the mind from its hidden divine root.

The Passing of the Veils ceremony is therefore an intense, religiously inspired, allegory, which is of major importance in understanding the Royal Arch Degree. The Passing of the Veils symbolizes the power and glory of the spiritual insights of the Royal Arch Degree. As the Blue Lodge stresses man's relationship to man, so the Chapter Degrees emphasize man's relationship to Deity. This is a profound and significant difference.

CONCLUSIONS

In the United States, the Passing of the Veils is an integral part of the Royal Arch Degree. In England, as part of the move away from Trinitarian Christian ritual, the Passing of the Veils was virtually eliminated. The ceremony continues to be practiced in Scotland and Ireland and the Irish ceremony bears considerable similarity to the American ceremony. The Passing of the Veils also exists in other areas in which Masonry was influenced by Britain, such as in Canada and Australia. The ceremony was brought back in Bristol, England in the very early part of the 20th century. However, there has not been any move to bring it back elsewhere in England. The Passing of the Veils is not only a beautiful degree, but conveys the rich spiritual message of the mystical Masonic journey to illumination and enlightenment.

BIBLIOGRAPHY AND CREDITS

Barker, M.: *Beyond the Veil of the Temple. The High Priestly Origin of the Apocalypses.* http://www.marquette.edu/maqom/veil.

Barker, R. J.: A Private Lodge Royal Arch Certificate. *Ars Quatuor Coronatorum.*111: 146–155, 1998

Carlile, R.: *Manual of Freemasonry.* Reeves and Turner.

Carr, H.: *Harry Carr's World of Freemasonry.* Lewis, 1983.

Chevalier, J. and Gheerbrandt, A., Tr. Buchanan-Brown, J. *The Penguin Dictionary of Symbols.* 2nd ed. Penguin, 1996.

Cook, E. H.: The Origin of the Ceremony known as Passing the Veils as Practiced in the Bristol Province. *Ars Quatuor Coronatorum.* 85: 325–330, 1972.

Hamill, J. M. English Royal Arch MS. Rituals c. 1780-c. 1830. *Ars Quatuor Coronatorum.* 95: 37–54, 1982.

Hawkyard, W. H. and Worts, F. R.: The Ceremony of "Passing the Veils". *Ars Quatuor Coronatorum.* 62: 186–193, 1951.

Jones, B. E.: *Freemasons' Book of the Royal Arch.* Revised Impression. Harrap, 1969.

Josephus, F.: *The Antiquities of the Jews. The New Complete Works of Josephus.* Tr. Whiston, W. Kregel, 1999.

The King James Bible.

Mackey, A. G.: *Encyclopedia of Freemasonry.* New Edition. The Masonic History Company. 1946.

Mendoza, H.: The Masonic Qualifications for the Royal Arch. *Ars Quatuor Coronatorum.* 96: 47–64, 1983

Supreme Grand Chapter of Queensland. *Elements of the Excellent Master Degree.* Module RA-4-EMM-IJW-09.05.99. 1999.

Thomas, A. J. B.: A Brief History of the Royal Arch in England. *Ars Quatuor Coronatorum.* 88:349–358, 1972.

Turnbull, E. R. and Denslow, R. V.: *A History of Royal Arch Masonry.* Reprinted Edition. Anchor, 1993.

Ward, E.: Richard Blake, The Royal York Lodge of Bristol and its R. A. and K. T. Appendages. Ars *Quatuor Coronatorum.* 79: 79–82, 1961.

Wells, R. A.: The Premier Grand Lodge and the Delayed Recognition of the Royal Arch. *Ars Quatuor Coronatorum.* 82: 74–100, 1969.

This article was originally published in Royal Arch Mason and was delivered as the 2005 Grand Historian Lecture, The Most Excellent Grand Chapter of Royal Arch Masons of Florida.

THE SIX MASONIC SONS OF GEORGE III

◆

BY MARTIN CHERRY

George III (1738–1820) is probably best known for his long reign, his "madness" and for losing the American War of Independence. However, Freemasons should remember him for other reasons.

George III was the grandson of George II and the son of Frederick Lewis, Prince of Wales (1707–1751), the first Royal Freemason. Frederick Lewis led a hedonistic lifestyle and died before his father, thrusting George III onto the thrones of England and Hanover in 1760 at the age of just 20.

A year later he married Princess Charlotte of Mecklenburg-Strelitz and fathered 15 children in 22 years. George III, unlike George I and George II, was popular with his English subjects. Born in England, he spoke English and preferred to live in England. Unlike his father, he was prudent, Tory, interested in agriculture, and according to Georgian society, the ruler of the dullest court in Europe.

This was also in marked contrast to his brothers, who like Frederick Lewis, enjoyed parties, drinking, gambling and running up huge debts. Three of George's brothers followed Frederick Lewis into Freemasonry, including Henry, Duke of Cumberland (1745–1790) who, in 1782, became Grand Master of the Premier Grand Lodge of England. George III never became a Freemason himself. However, he did father seven sons who lived to maturity, of whom six became Freemasons. Those six sons were: George, Prince of Wales; Frederick Augustus, Duke of York; William Henry, Duke of Clarence; Edward Augustus, Duke of Kent; Ernest Augustus, Duke of Cumberland; and Augustus Frederick, Duke of Sussex.

They were men of very differing characters, with contrasting political and personal outlooks on life, but all found something in Freemasonry, which is why they are all worth examining as individual men and Freemasons.

George, Prince of Wales

The Prince of Wales, later Prince Regent and in 1820 King George IV, was born in 1762 and died in 1830. The position of Prince of Wales is a difficult one, especially when your father lives to 82. George was an intelligent child with lots of promise, but quickly became a cause for concern to his father and the country.

Unlike most of his brothers, George was denied a military career which he longed for as a young man. He quickly fell in with people of whom his father disapproved, such as the Whig politician Charles Fox and, more importantly to Freemasons, his uncle, Henry.

Cumberland and his circle introduced George to the pleasures of drink, gambling and the theatre. By 1785 George had married the Catholic actress Maria Fitzherbert. The marriage was illegal because of the Royal Marriage Act, which meant that all Royal marriages needed the consent of both the King and Parliament and that marriage to Catholics was forbidden. Mrs. Fitzherbert had to be paid off by the government, but continued to be the Prince's mistress for many years.

In 1787, at a special Lodge meeting held at the Star and Garter in Pall Mall, George was initiated into Freemasonry by his uncle Henry. That year, George formed his own Lodge, The Prince of Wales's Lodge (now No. 259). Initially the members were a mixture of his friends and household such as Chevalier Ruspini, his dentist—one of the founders of the Royal Masonic Institute for Girls—and Louis Weltje, the Prince's chief cook.

The Lodge attracted other high-ranking Masons such as Thomas Dunckerley and the Tory Prime Minister George Canning. At this stage, George was still a popular figure in Britain and his association with Freemasonry would have given further respectability to Grand Lodge.

Therefore, it was not surprising that George was elected Grand Master on the death of his uncle in 1790. George was not the most active of Grand Masters. He enjoyed the social side of Freemasonry, and its imagery found its way into some of the designs at the Royal Pavilion in Brighton.

He also had an able Acting Grand Master in the Earl of Moira. As the Prince of Wales's private and public life became more complicated, his involvement in the Craft diminished. He married Caroline of Brunswick in 1795, who provided him with a daughter, Charlotte, in 1796 and spent the rest of her life in conflict with her husband.

The Grand Lodge of Scotland elected George as Grand Master in 1805, but there is no evidence that he ever attended a Lodge, let alone Grand Lodge, north of the border.

In 1811 the King's illness (porphyria) that had been troubling him since the 1780s, forced him out of public life and George IV became Regent.

By 1813 his involvement with Freemasonry had come to an end, although he was given the title Grand Patron of the Order. The Prince Regent became George IV in 1820. As King he abandoned liberal politics and became very reactionary. In the end he became best known for his indulgences, his womanising and his girth, although perhaps he should also be remembered for his patronage of the arts and architecture, and to Freemasons for being the first of their order to become King of England.

Frederick Augustus, Duke of York

Born in 1763 and created Bishop of Osnabruck in Hanover at the age of seven months, Frederick was George III's favourite son. Initially educated with his older brother George, Frederick was a bright student and was later sent to Prussia to train for a military career.

In 1784 he married Princess Frederica of Prussia and was created Duke of York. Frederick and the Prince of Wales were firm friends, often drinking and womanising together, and the Duke of York became a Mason in the same year as his older brother. He was initiated in Britannic Lodge (now No. 33), which also met at the Star and Garter and was made a Past Grand Master of the Premier Grand Lodge soon after. Naturally, he joined his brother's Lodge.

In 1789 he fought a duel with Lieutenant-Colonel Lennox, who had insulted the Prince of Wales. The duel was a bit of a Masonic affair, the Earl of Moira was Frederick's second and Lennox, who survived the duel after the Prince refused to shoot, later went on to become Duke of Richmond and Provincial Grand Master of Sussex. For a number of years the Prince of Wales's Lodge held an annual celebration to honour Frederick's courage.

Like his older brother, Frederick's life was not short of scandal. His military career was chequered. In 1793, revolutionary France had invaded Holland and Frederick was placed in command of the British forces by his father. His campaign, which was hindered by bad advice from older generals, could have defeated France before the rise of Napoleon, but his strategy of constant repositioning of troops led to Frederick becoming the subject of the nursery rhyme "The Grand Old Duke of York" after a second failed campaign in 1798.

Frederick did, however, as Commander-in-Chief, transform the organisation of the army, improve the training of soldiers, especially officers, with the establishment of military academies, and insist on better equipment and supplies for the men in the field.

Unfortunately, his military career came to an end in 1809, after one of his mistresses, Mrs Clarke, accused him of selling commissions. Although cleared by a parliamentary enquiry, he resigned his position. On his death in 1827, grateful soldiers raised the funds to build a statue of him, which still stands today at Carlton Terrace in London.

William Henry, Duke of Clarence

George's third son William, born in 1765, was sent to sea at the age of 13 to become a Midshipman. William took to Navy life. He was involved in the capture of a Spanish convoy in 1779, was thrown in the brig for brawling in Gibraltar, and visited New York in 1781 at the height of the War of Independence.

He became a friend of Nelson and gave away the bride at Nelson's wedding in 1787. He was the first of the six brothers to be made a Mason in 1786, joining Prince George Lodge No. 86 in Plymouth. This Lodge, which was comprised of naval and army officers, was erased in 1828. As with his brothers, he was made a Past Grand Master. He took a keen interest in Freemasonry, joining the Prince of Wales's Lodge, of which he became Master in 1827.

In 1790 he started a relationship with an actress, Dorothy Jordan, and fathered ten children by her, all with the surname Fitzclarence. His naval career petered out during the Napoleonic wars, and in 1818 he settled down to marry Princess Adelaide of Saxe-Meiningen. They had two daughters but neither survived.

On the death of George IV in 1830, William became King William IV. He reigned for only seven years, but presided over some major changes to the British political system including the Reform Bills of 1831 and 1832, which led to the demise of rotten or pocket boroughs.

William gave up Freemasonry when he became king. Prince of Wales's Lodge members were given permission to line their aprons with garter blue to mark his accession, and his brother Augustus Frederick succeeded him as Master of the Lodge.

Edward Augustus, Duke of Kent

Edward (1767–1820) was, like his brothers, Frederick and Ernest, destined for a military life. As a soldier he was known as a strict disciplinarian who sometimes treated his men too harshly, but outside of the army he was interested in liberal politics, social reform and charities. The early socialist Robert Owen was among his circle of friends.

His military training took him to Geneva, where in 1789 he was initiated into Masonry in the Loge Union des Cours of the Grand Orient of Geneva. It was also in Geneva where he met the French noblewoman Julie de St. Laurent, who became his mistress and companion for 28 years.

In 1790 he was placed in command of the garrison in Gibraltar and the Moderns used this as an opportunity to make him Provincial Grand Master there. Edward had two unsuccessful postings running the Gibraltar garrison.

His policy of closing public houses and confining the men to barracks when there was little to do, led to two mutinies and his withdrawal by the Duke of York. In 1791 he was stationed in Quebec with his regiment, the Royal Fusiliers, and he spent the next nine years in Canada and the West Indies.

Edward was still unpopular with his men, but socially with the local population he and Madam St. Laurent proved a success. During this period Edward agreed to become Provincial Grand Master for Lower Canada for the rival Antients Grand Lodge.

It is not known why Edward decided to join the Antients, but his decision to do so would be significant for both Grand Lodges. He certainly helped the cause of the Antients in Canada. In 1791 there were only three Antients lodges in Canada, but there were 20 by 1813, some of which had switched allegiance from the Moderns.

In 1794 he expressed his desire to see the unification of the two rival Grand Lodges. He was made Duke of Kent in 1798 and returned to England in 1800. His interest in Freemasonry extended to other Orders, and from 1804–1806 he was Grand Master of the Knights Templar.

In 1813 the Duke of Atholl, who had also been keen on unification, stepped down as Grand Master of the Antients Grand Lodge and Edward took his place. With his brother the Duke of Sussex as Grand Master of the Moderns, unification took place and the United Grand Lodge of England was born at the end of 1813.

It was about this time that Edward's involvement in Masonry stopped. In 1817 the Prince of Wales's daughter had died and public pressure was put on the other brothers to produce an heir to the throne to succeed the Prince Regent. Madam St. Laurent retired to a nunnery in 1818 and the Duke of Kent married Princess Victoria of Saxe-Coburg. By 1820, the year of Edward's death he had fathered a daughter, Princess Alexandrina Victoria, who the world would later know as Queen Victoria.

Ernest Augustus, Duke of Cumberland

Born in 1771, Ernest Augustus became the black sheep of the family, which was no mean feat considering the reputation of most of his brothers. Initially things looked good for Ernest. He was tall, fit, handsome and destined to do great things in the Hanoverian cavalry, which he joined in 1791.

By 1792 he was a Colonel in the Hanoverian Dragoons and eventually rose to the rank of Field Marshal. In 1793 he was wounded in action whilst fighting under the Duke of York's command.

At this point in his life everything was going well. The Earl of Moira, Acting Grand Master and another military Mason, initiated the Prince at a special Lodge in 1796 at the Earl's house. He was immediately made a Past Grand Master and joined Britannic Lodge two years later.

In 1799 Parliament made him Duke of Cumberland when he married Princess Frederica of Mecklenberg-Strelitz. Unfortunately, from this point his reputation in Britain began to suffer a series of setbacks. Rumours began to circulate in the British press and society about the Duke.

His sister, the unmarried Princess Sophia, had a child in 1800 and Cumberland was believed to be the father, when in fact it was General Thomas Garth, who later brought up the child. In 1810, one of Ernest's servants Sellis tried to kill the Duke with a sword, giving him a near fatal head wound, and then committed suicide.

Rumour had it that the Duke was either having an affair with Sellis' wife or with Sellis, but neither could be proven. He was accused of assaulting the wife of the Chancellor, Lord Lyndhurst, when in fact they had only argued about politics and, in 1829, Lord Graves killed himself when he was told Ernest was having an affair with his wife.

This rumour was again untrue, but Ernest's character and actions did not endear him to the public. He preferred Hanover and made that quite obvious to everyone. In 1827 he became Grand Master of the Orange Order at a time when Parliament was condemning it for its bad effect on Irish politics. He opposed

Catholic emancipation, even trying to form his own Tory government, but was defeated by the Whigs and the majority of the Tories led by Wellington.

He lined up against the Reform Bills with the Tories in the House of Lords against his brother the Duke of Sussex, who was a Whig. Disgruntled, Ernest spent less and less time in England. He had joined Lodge Frederick of the White Horse (Hanover) in 1813 and became Grand Master of the Grand Lodge of Hanover in 1828. In 1837, on the death of William IV, Ernest became King of Hanover, as Victoria was ineligible as a woman.

True to form, Ernest scrapped Hanover's liberal constitution and set about ruling the country as an absolute monarch. He died in 1851, handing the throne to his blind son George, who was deposed after 15 years when Hanover was annexed by Prussia.

Augustus Frederick, Duke of Sussex

The Duke of Sussex stands tall over English Freemasonry. He was born in 1773, the ninth child and sixth son of George III. Augustus, who was educated abroad, was supposed to follow his brother William into the navy, but he had severe asthma, so avoided military service altogether.

His father tried to keep him abroad, firstly for his health and secondly to avoid English women who might lead him astray. George failed and Augustus met Lady Augusta Murray on a trip to Rome in 1792. Against the Royal Marriage Act, they secretly married and later had two children. The eldest child, Augustus Frederick d'Este, would eventually become a Past Junior Grand Warden in the United Grand Lodge of England.

Augustus was probably the most liberal of the sons. Like his brother Edward, he involved himself in Whig politics, social reform and charity work. He was also interested in languages, art and science. He became a Freemason whilst in Berlin, joining the Lodge Victorious Truth in 1798.

Once back in England he joined the Prince of Wales's Lodge in 1800. He really took to Freemasonry, joining the Lodge of Friendship No. 6 in 1806, the Lodge of Antiquity No. 2 in 1808 and Royal Alpha Lodge No. 16 in 1820. By 1820 he was Master of all these Lodges.

In 1810 he became Grand Principal of the Grand and Royal Chapter, in 1812 Deputy Grand Master and in 1813 succeeded the Prince Regent as the Grand Master of the Premier Grand Lodge of England. For a number of years senior Masons in the two rival Grand Lodges had been negotiating behind the scenes for unification. When the Articles of Union were signed by the two Dukes, Kent and

Sussex, Augustus described it as the happiest day of his life. Augustus Frederick, Duke of Sussex was now Grand Master of the United Grand Lodge of England, a position he would hold to his death in 1843.

He exercised strong leadership over the newly united Grand Lodge. He took measures to reinforce the Union, such as establishing the Lodge of Reconciliation to regulate the ritual and placing emphasis on the Craft degrees and the Royal Arch rather than allowing expansion of the additional degrees.

His liberal attitude towards religion (he was in favour of Catholic Emancipation and had many Jewish friends), influenced the creation of a more inclusive, less obviously Christian Grand Lodge. He was a dedicated attendee at Grand Lodge, even when his eyesight and health was failing and he saw the United Grand Lodge through its infancy.

In his public life he continued to back charities and social reform. He built up a huge library, which landed him in debt, a situation he shared with all his brothers with the exception of Ernest. He supported Catholic Emancipation and the Reform Bill despite most of his older brothers' opposition.

He illegally married again in 1831 to Celia Underwood and in 1840 he gave away Queen Victoria at her wedding to Prince Albert. He died in 1843 and was widely mourned in both the Masonic and the non-Masonic world. In 1846, a six-ton statue by Edward Hodges Bailey RA was erected in the Grand Temple at Freemasons' Hall. The statue now dominates the Sussex corridor of the current Freemasons' Hall in Great Queen Street, a little like the man himself.

The seventh son of George III was Adolphus Frederick. He was born in 1774 and died in 1850. In 1801 he was given the title Duke of Cambridge, and after a military career, acted as Governor of Hanover until his brother Ernest became King. It is unknown why he did not follow his brothers into the Craft.

Selected reading

Fulford, Roger: *Royal Dukes: the father and uncles of Queen Victoria* (London: 1933)
Van der Kiste: *George III's Children* (Stroud: 1992)

The Library and Museum of the United Grand Lodge of England has a free information sheet giving details of the Masonic careers of all Royal Freemasons which is available on request.

This article was based on an informal talk by Martin Cherry, Assistant Librarian (now Librarian), as part of the Library and Museum of Freemasonry's Spring 2004 talks programme.

STONE: ITS SYMBOLISM AND INFLUENCE IN WORLD CULTURE AND FREEMASONRY

◆

BY PETER J. MILLHEISER, MD, FACS

Why stone? What was the reason for selecting stone as the symbolic vehicle of Freemasonry? What was the rationale for constructing a major social, quasi-religious, moral, and intellectual movement based on the work of seemingly barely literate skilled laborers? What caused Goethe and Mozart to create works of unsurpassed inspiration based on the Freemasonry? The underlying thread in the basic foundation of Freemasonry is after all the symbolism of stone. To fully understand Freemasonry, it is necessary to have an appreciation of the universal symbolic importance that stone has had on society since the dawn of history. Stone and symbolism are two of the major ongoing motifs in Freemasonry.

G. S. Shepherd-Jones in a pamphlet *From Craft to Arch* gave an excellent and concise summation of the importance of Masonic symbolism. It is not generally realized that Freemasonry consists not just of rituals and ceremonies but that some of its most beautiful truths are contained in Masonic symbols. Masonic symbolism consists of

> … texts without commentaries, mute expressions of a spiritual language, concealing more than they first reveal.… [Without understanding these symbols] we shall never experience the full force of Freemasonry, with all its comprehensive teachings of moral and religious truths.[1]

The symbolism of stone has had an incredibly powerful hold on the imagination of man through the millennia. Stone has been used as the allegorical basis not only of Freemasonry, but of many religious rituals and folk customs dating back some 40,000 years to Paleolithic times.

> I have a word of secret to tell thee,
>   a message to whisper unto thee:
> It is a contraption that launches words,
>   a Stone that whispers.
> Men its messages will not know;
> Earth's multitudes will not comprehend.
>
> Heaven with Earth it makes converse,
>   and the seas with the planets.
> It is a Stone of Splendor;
> To heaven it is yet unknown.
> Let's you and I raise it
>   within my cavern, on lofty Zaphon.[2]

Ancient Canaanite Ugarit tablet found at <u>Rash Shamra</u>

The impact of stone on the imagination has been such that workers with stone were selected to form the allegorical basis of Freemasonry. In his outstanding study of Masonic symbols, Zeldis noted that by studying the rich symbolism of stone, we can illuminate many aspects of Freemasonry in order to develop a fuller understanding of its rituals and traditions.[3] Workers with wood could just as easily have been chosen and their tools similarly used to convey important spiritual concepts. What made Freemasonry choose the medium of stone for their religious allegories?

Many other symbols were used by fraternal organizations to represent their philosophy. The Society of Free Gardeners, which was a similar fraternal society, based their philosophy on the symbolism of flowers as the route to spiritual perfection. Durr has reviewed the extensive use of what we understand to be Masonic symbols which were published in emblem books beginning in the sixteenth century and which were widely used by various guilds and crafts and by other fraternal societies. In the emblem books, tools were widely used as icons to demonstrate moral messages.[4] Yet, there is something special in stone; stone has some inherent and intrinsic essence that has given it a special power with deep philosophical implications since Paleolithic times which in turn has had a profound effect upon Freemasonry. A very significant import for Freemasonry lay in the medium upon which the workers practiced their art for stone had a special symbolic importance rather being simply an inanimate object.

THE LANGUAGE OF SYMBOLS

The language of symbols forms a type of universal language. Symbols have long been used as a means of expressing a hierophany, which is defined as the manifestation or display of a sacred mystery. A hierophany is the sudden irruption of the sacred into the profane world. It is a more widely applicable word that the older term, "theophany" which denotes the manifestation, appearance, or display of a god.[5] The use of symbols with their esoteric meanings transports us back through sacred time, as opposed to profane time, to the very origins of man. The shared meaning of stone from prehistoric times to our own demonstrates a universal cross-cultural human society with stone as one of its principal unifying motifs. This linkage will be shown to date back to Neanderthal man. This hierophany of stone has been structurally similar throughout history. It becomes a universal sacralization of reality.

Symbols possess esoteric meanings which are often not readily apparent. The goldfinch is a one of many recurring symbols in Renaissance art. The theme of the Madonna shown with Jesus holding a goldfinch was found in Raphael's *Madonna del Cardellino* in the *Uffizi,* in which the infant Jesus plays with a goldfinch. The goldfinch was alleged by legend to have pulled a thorn from the head of Jesus during the crucifixion and this scene was therefore regarded as a divine premonition of the Passion. The same motif was painted by many other artists including Albrecht Durer and Giabattista Tiepolo.

This particular symbolism of the goldfinch was also used in the beautiful, meditative piano composition *Vingt Regards sur l'Enfant-Jesus* (Twenty Contemplations of the Infant Jesus) by the twentieth century composer Oliver Messiaen, which included the song of the goldfinch as part of the divine mystery Thus, as common a creature as a song bird could be symbolic of a divine mystery which lies at the heart of the faith of a billion people. Similarly, stone will be shown to have had this powerful impact on societies around the world for almost 40,000 years.

BASIC SYMBOLISM OF STONE

Stone has a unique symbolism which far transcends its outward appearance. It was regarded by primitive man as possessing great sacred and spiritual values and the symbolic meaning of stone has not only continued to the present but is even quite prominently expressed in the current cultural world.

Carl Jung explored the concept of the inherent magical and religious power of stone as an important part of the functioning of the brain as well as of the soul. To Jung, the alchemical stone was something eternal which alchemists compared to the mystical feeling of finding God within your soul.[6]

Mircea Eliade offered a further understanding of the attraction of stone and the fascination that its majestic power and force brings to man. Permanence in matter bought a religious consciousness to primitive man and nothing was more awe-inspiring than a majestic rock or piece of granite. Rock transcended the precariousness of one's being and its strength helped make it something that was superhuman. Rock alternately fascinated, terrified, and attracted man. Its grandeur confronted man with a reality and force that belonged to a world other than the profane world of which he was a part.[7]

Throughout time, various naturally occurring objects have been interpreted as hierophanies, or manifestations of a sacred mystery. These objects included rocks, mountains, the dawn, the sun, trees, and waterfalls. This was a naturally occurring and virtually universal language and culture of symbols. The primordial flood, the rising sun (banishing darkness and death), Creation stories, the birth of the hero, death and resurrection stories, hope of a future life, salvation, light as the antidote to death and darkness, the central mountain symbolized as the great temple, the *axis mundi* or central axis of the universe, the *omphalos* or the stone which symbolically is the center of the earth, ritual ceremonies for the pubescent male, decoration of the skin, and sex-linked methods of addressing people are all a part of this universal language of symbolism. These symbols link us today with the advent of recorded history.

STONE IN EARLY SOCIETIES

The children of Adam's son Seth were said by Josephus in the *Jewish Antiquities* to be the inventors of that peculiar type of wisdom which is concerned with the heavenly bodies and their order. Based on a prediction by Adam that the world would be destroyed at one time by fire and at another time by flood, they made two pillars, one of brick and one of stone and inscribed their discoveries on both. These pillars were reputed by Josephus to be "in the land of Siriad to this day."[8]

Cosmological concepts of stone common in primitive cultures have combined with the numerous references to stone in the Bible to make more understandable the allegories of Freemasonry.

Stone was regarded by early man as having a life force rather than being simply inanimate matter. It represented something beyond itself which gave it a sacred meaning as an instrument of spiritual action.[9] Stone was felt to fall to the earth from the heavens. Quartz was splinters falling from the sky.[10] There were myths that mineral ores were stones which gestated in mother earth.[11] Native Americans observed the mysterious petrified fossils and tried to understand how extinct animals had been transformed into apparent stone by creating legends about the origin of these creatures.

Among the Indians of the Northwest coast, there was an initiation ceremony, described by Franz Boas, into a secret society called the *Tlokaola* into which the novice was supposedly initiated by wolves. The novice would be seized and carried off into the woods at night by members of the tribe wearing wolf masks. He would be brought back the next day supposedly dead and would have to be revived by the members of the society. The "wolves" were alleged to have placed a magic stone inside his body and two wizards or shamans would then remove the stone bringing the novice back to life.[12]

Stone was also felt to be symbolic of the Earth Mother and stones heaped into vertical piles were symbolic of the central mountain or *axis mundi* stretching from the center of the earth towards heaven. Hermes was referred to as the God of Stones and was represented by piles of stones or herms.[13] Piled up stones also have other symbolic meanings. Jews will leave individual stones on a tombstone when they visit a grave as a sign of respect. The broken stone column, which is an important symbol of the Master Mason Degree, symbolizes the death of man. Burial megaliths were used to mark tombs and in India were thought to fasten down and provide a temporary dwelling place for a dead person's soul so that it could influence the fertility of the fields but not be able to roam about or become dangerous. This protected the living against the dead. Stone was therefore a symbolic habitat of the spirit of the dead.[14]

Menhirs were megaliths or giant stones and were upright oblong stones similar to unhewn or unfinished obelisks and were prevalent in Western Europe from the Neolithic Period on. They were primarily burial structures similar to the table-like dolmens of Brittany and the *Hünengräber* or giant's graves of northern Germany. The menhirs may have had a phallic fertility role similar to the Indian lingam or may have served as "seats for the soul" or simply been markers of a sacred place. As tomb Guardians, they would have been placed near or over burial sites as stone was regarded as an incorruptible substance. Near Carnac in Brittany are fields of aligned megaliths which may have had an astronomical purpose similar to those in Stonehenge in England. They may also have served as part of a symbolic religious system of which we have no knowledge.[15] Serving a probably similar function to menhirs were the dolmens of Britain and France which consisted of a large flat horizontal stone set on 2 large vertical stone slabs and may have once been covered with earth, serving as a burial chamber. Dolmens are often found in close proximity to menhirs.

Stone was something hard and permanent in contrast to the impermanence of biological life. It was worshiped as not only representing deity but also as being an earthly residence of deity. The god Mithra existed inside a stone prior to his birth. The Mithraic temples were therefore built to resemble caves analogous to wombs of stone.[16] There is a Caucasian tradition, "In the beginning, the world was covered with water. The Great creator-god dwelt inside a rock." The Kaa'ba in Saudi Arabia, which is probably a meteorite, is venerated by Muslims to this day. The Black Stone of Pessinus represented the Phrygian Great Mother goddess.[17]

Zosimos of Panopolis (circa 300 C.E.), an Egyptian alchemist, quoted a Persian alchemist, Ostanes, who wrote:

> Go to the waters of the Nile and there you will find a stone that has a spirit (*pneuma*). Take this, divide it, thrust it in your hand and draw out its heart: for the soul (*psyche*) is in its heart.

The search for this stone, the *lapis philosophorum*, or the philosopher's stone, the stone which could convert base metals into gold, would occupy the efforts of alchemists for at least 1,500 years.[18] This transmutation was analogous to the liberation of the soul from the body-tomb leading to the purification of the soul.

Precious stones were supposed by the ancients to have great magical powers and were initially worn as amulets rather than as jewelry.[19] In the Banks Islands, powerful ghosts lived in certain long stones and the ghosts could drain the soul from a person whose shadow fell across those stones.[20]

Stone had a magical protective power. The women of the island of Timor would bring out baskets containing fruits and stones. These would then be anointed to protect their warriors from bullets.[21] Various other magical properties were ascribed to stone in various societies. In Peru, stones were used to improve the growth of crops and to increase the number of cattle. In Melanesia, various shapes of stones held spirits dwelling within them with magical powers. If you found a stone found with smaller stones beneath it would cause you to find pigs. A stone found with other specific markings on it would bring you money. From ancient times, certain stones in Greece and Albania could insure an adequate flow of milk in nursing mothers. In Greece, a particular stone could cure snake-bite.[22]

Frazer's *The Golden Bough* has an extensive survey of stone's ability to bring on rain. Throughout Australia, stones are used in ceremonies for rain-making. At Sagami in Japan, there is a stone which will cause rain to fall if water is poured on it. In central Africa, the Wawamba tribe has a rain-stone which, when anointed with oil and then placed in a pot of water, will cause rain to fall. The Apaches of the American southwest poured water from a certain spring onto a rock to cause rain. In Dulyn or the Black Lake in Snowdon in Wales, there were stepping stones leading from high and dangerous rocks into the lake. If one could walk far enough into the lake on the stones to be able to throw water to reach and wet the furthest stone called the Red Altar, there would be rain. In Breton in France, throwing water from a fountain in the woods, near where the wizard Merlin sleeps, on a stone slab will cause rain. Outside the walls of Rome near a temple of Mars, there was a stone, the *lapis manalis*. When a drought occurred, this stone would be dragged into Rome causing rain immediately to fall.

The pagan practices of the rain-stone were Christianized by the practice of dipping stone crosses into water and by the French and Spanish custom of dipping images of saints into water. The Buddhist Shan people of southeastern Asia will similarly wet images of Buddha for the same purpose. The Yakut tied a stone to a stick and waved it about to bring about a hot day. In Scotland, wind was caused by beating a wet rag against a stone.[23]

The transformation of man into stone has existed since ancient times. The early Native Americans regarded the petrified fossil remains of prehistoric dinosaurs and birds as great monsters which had been turned into stone. The Salish people of British Columbia regarded many geographical places as ancestors who had been transformed into stone or some other permanent physical feature of the area. The life-force of these powerful ancestors was felt to be in the rocks and bodies of water of the area, with the power of the transformed person filling these places. These rocks and cliff sides where ancestors were turned to stone, had the ability to cause changes in the weather.[24]

Stone was also used as a means of punishment not only for moral sins but also for ritual punishment. In ancient Greece, a scapegoat would be chosen and stoned to death to avoid plague, famine, or drought.[25] In biblical times, stoning was the punishment for moral infractions.

Stone also served as a means of communication from deity to man. There were speaking stones which had fallen from heaven and these had the power of divine prophecy and were to be found at the oracle shrines such as at Delphi.[26]

Stones were considered to have human functions. In Vietnam, a stone will bleed if struck by a pick. Stone also had medicinal functions. Pliny mentions that among the ancient Greeks, a certain stone could cure jaundice as its hue resembled the skin color of the jaundiced patient.[27] In many societies throughout the world, people would strike themselves with stones and then discard the stones as a way of getting rid of fatigue.[28] St. Jerome is often painted striking his chest with a rock to drive out impure thoughts as an act of contrition.

The steadfastness of stone was an important symbol in early societies. The early Danish historian, Saxo Grammaticus, noted that the people met to vote for a king, they stood on stones to symbolize that this deed would be long-lasting.[29] Stone also was an important part of coronation ceremonies. The Stone of Scone was originally associated with the coronation of the Scottish Kings. It was moved to England and was placed under the coronation chair in Westminster Abbey. In Ireland, the "stone of knowledge", standing on a hill in mystical Tara, would cry out when touched by the rightful king. Nearby were reputed to be two stones so close together that a man could not pass through them. When they accepted a man as the future king, the two stones would move apart to let his carriage through.[30] Other stones served as a means of communication between the seer and the god. The sibyl carried a stone with her and would sit on it when making prophecies.[31]

THE FERTILITY POWER OF STONE

Stone also symbolized fertility as the earth-mother endowed with the ability to bring forth life in addition to having other human physiological traits. Semitic traditions contain accounts of humans being born from a stone and in some Christian legends, Christ was born of a stone.

This tradition was also found in China in the *Huai-nan-tzu* which proclaimed that the legendary and semi-divine Yü, the first Hsia Dynasty Emperor, was born from a stone. Kao Yu in the 2nd century wrote that Yü's mother was moved [to pregnancy] by a stone and bore Yü. Another tradition stated that Yü's mother dreamed of a meteorite (which has a stony essence) and similarly was moved [to pregnancy]. K'i, Yü's son was also said to have been born from a stone. Yü was the cultural hero who was also regarded as divine and in the *Huai-nan-tzu,* he was referred to as the consecrated *She* deity. In the *She* temples, the stone was worshipped as embodying the deity of the temple. Kao Mei, the divine matchmaker, who was a procreative deity, had a stone placed at the altar in her temples. This reflected the alliance of stone with divine and procreative power and tied together the link between stone, fertility, and procreation. Nü-kua, a Chinese goddess of match-making and birth-giving, was closely linked with the altar stone. T'u-shan was turned into a stone which then gave birth to the royal line and was the tribal mother of the Hsia people. T'u-shan was the first reference in Chinese culture to the concrete image of the child-bearing stone.[32] It is likely that the concept of regeneration of life embodied in the concept of the alchemist's Philosopher's Stone came from this tradition.[33]

In other traditions, stones have given birth to precious stones. In addition to stone being the residence of deity and an aniconic representation of deity, it also had a feminine and maternal connotation. Fertility was a major aspect of the power resident in certain stones. Early societies regarded stones and rocks as the source of human life. There were numerous accounts of gods being born from stone as well as the first man.

Ovid's *Metamorphoses* describes how when the mythic Deucalion and Pyrrha sought to repopulate the earth following a great mythic flood which had destroyed mankind, the goddess Themis advised them to throw the bones of the Great Mother over their head behind them. Understanding that the bones of the Great Mother meant stones in the body of the earth, they proceeded to throw stones back over their head. The stones softened and assumed human form. The stones thrown by Deucalion became men and those thrown by Pyrrha became women.[34]

The Phrygian sky god, Papas fell asleep on the Agdos rock which had assumed the shape of the great mother goddess, Cybele. His semen fell on the rock and fertilized it and a savage being, Agdistis, was born. The rock out of which Arthur pulls his sword is also the maternal rock that is analogous to Jesus' tomb or Mithra's birth cave or the altar on which Isaac is nearly sacrificed. The Australian Aborigines have a legend in which a huge rock, Erathipa, has the souls of children inside and there is an opening in the rock from which the souls can escape and enter into the wombs of women walking by the rock and be reborn.[35]

There were numerous legends of women who would rub themselves against certain rocks in order to conceive children. The vital energy contained within the rock was transferred into the pelvis of a woman enhancing her fertility. The custom of "sliding" in which a woman who wanted a child would slide on a certain stone was widespread. There was a huge rock called the Stone Mare at Saint-Renan (Finisterre) upon which a woman who wanted a child would sleep for three nights. Young brides would come there for the first few nights after their weddings and rub their bellies against it. Other stones could insure that a woman would have a male child. The flat stone on the top of the dolmen was felt to be able to store up energy from the earth and pass the heat or life force along to infertile women who sat on the stone.[36]

Until one hundred years ago, women in London would clasp the pillars of Saint Paul's Cathedral to enable them to have children. Touching certain stones could make a sterile woman fertile and other stones could also insure a good delivery for the baby.[37] In Gabon, placing a stone axe thunderstone between the legs of a woman in labor would ease childbirth. Yakut women, after a baby's birth, drank water with chips of this type of stone to facilitate delivery of the placenta.[38]

Among the Dyaks of Borneo, when a woman was having a difficult labor, a medicine man outside the room would attach a large stone to his abdomen with a cloth and manipulate it to simulate the movements of the baby in labor until the baby finally was born.[39]

Standing upright stones such as the boulder-like menhirs or the Hindu lingams were fertility symbols. In Brittany, women would rub their bellies with the stone dust from the menhirs as well as with the moisture that collected on its rough surface. Stones with holes in them through which hands or legs or even bodies could pass through symbolized the birth passage and were also fertility symbols.[40]

Isaiah also expresses the concept of people being born or hewn from rock.

> Hearken to me, ye that follow after righteousness, ye that seek the Lord: look into the rock whence you are hewn, and into the hole whence ye are digged.
>
> Isaiah 51: 1

THE POWER AND SACRED NATURE OF STONE

Not only was stone a powerful symbol of fertility, birth, and regeneration but the spiritual heavenly Jerusalem itself was encrusted with precious stones.

> And the building of the wall of it was of jasper: and the city was pure gold, like unto clear glass. And the foundations of the wall of the city were garnished with all manner of precious stones. The first foundation was jasper; the second, sapphire; the third a chalcedony; the fourth, an emerald; the fifth, a sardonyx; the sixth, sardius; the seventh. chrysolite; the eight, beryl; the ninth, a topaze; the tenth a chrysoprasus; the eleventh, a jacinth; the twelfth, an amethyst. And the twelve gates were twelve pearls ... and the street of the city was of pure gold ...
>
> Revelation 21: 18–21

What is apparent is that stone itself is not the entity to be worshipped. Stone is instead a means for worship containing a sacred mystery within. In various societies around the world, stone was the dwelling place of deity, but stone itself was not a deity. Certain stones could allow the sacred mystery of fertilization to occur, but this was only the expression of a specific innate power within a particular stone and did not apply to stone in general.

Michelangelo believed that his sculpture involved releasing what was already contained within the rock. His sculptures brought the creative force and power of stone to a level never before seen. In *The Boboli Slaves,* a series of unfinished sculptures of four bound captives in the Galleria dell'Accademia in Florence there is an incredible vitality and power of the stone from which each figure struggles to free himself. The encompassing rough stone tightly binds each figure in a powerful embrace and the stone is alive with its own vitality. It is the battle of man against the primordial forces binding him resulting in a cosmic release of energy similar to the energy release at the Creation. It is man in his most elemental form struggling into life.

In addition to the birth symbolism of stone, the symbolism of the stone pillars has important iconographic meanings. The stone pillars at the entrance to King Solomon's Temple had a specifically non-architectural meaning. They were pillars which did not support the building but whose symbolic purpose was described in their names, Jachin and Boaz or establishment and strength. The sacred nature of these pillars mirrored the usage of two pillars found at the entrance to various ancient Semitic temples such as the temple of Melkart at Tyre and the temples at Papphos and Hierapolis. The ancient temple at Megiddo had two quadrilateral stone columns at its entrance similar to those in the entrance of the place of sacrifice in the ancient Edomite sanctuary at Petra in Jordan.

The sacred nature of stone was especially important to the ancient Semites. Clement of Alexandria described the nomads of Syria and Arabia as "the Arabs who worship the stone." The sacred stone was an important part of the ancient Arabian worship.[41] A conical stone, which symbolically was a pillar, was worshipped as a symbol of the goddess Astarte. Obelisks had similarly sacred meanings. These stones manifested the divine presence and were the house of deity.

Dating back to antiquity, stone was used for sacrifice and the shedding of blood on the sacred altar was analogous to anointing it. Gradually, the altar and the sacred stones became two distinct entities and sacred stones would be erected around the altar. The sacred stones were found by the Israelites in the Canaanite sanctuaries and on the "high places" and were incorporated by them into their religious observances becoming memorials of events in the lives of the Patriarchs and in the history of the nation such as Jacob's stone at Bethel, Joshua's stone at Gilgal, and the stone Samuel set up between Mizpeh and Shen.[42]

The concept of the sacrificial nature of foundation stones was explored at length by G. W. Speth. There were two types of foundation stones. One was the actual physical stone anointed with a harmless substance such as oil. The second was the spiritual counterpart in which there was an actual sacrifice to provide a guardian spirit for the building. In many cases, the victim was the actual architect of the building, which may be of particular interest to Freemasons as this may have been the basis of the Masonic tradition of Hiram Abiff.[43] An interesting variation of this tradition can be found in Edgar Allan Poe's *The Cask of Amontillado*.

Stone was the foundation not only of altars but also of religions and it becomes the edifice of foundation of religion. For Jesus, Peter, whose name in Greek means stone, would be the foundation of the church.

> And I say also unto thee, that thou are Peter, and upon this rock I will build my church;
>
> Matthew 16: 18

Not only was stone the foundation of religion but it was regarded by the ancient Hebrews as the very foundation of the earth.

> Then the Lord answered Job out of the whirlwind and said ...
> Where wast thou when I laid the foundations of the earth?
> Declare if thou hath understanding.
> Who hath laid the measures thereof, if thou knowest?
> Or who laid the cornerstone thereof?
>
> Job 38: 1–4

If stone was the foundation of the earth and religion, it had to reflect this in the symbolism of the architecture of houses of worship. The religious symbolism of the Gothic style of churches, including the symbolism of stone, was described as early as the 1120's by Honorious of Autun.

> This House is set upon a stone foundation and the Church is founded on the sure rock of Christ ... The stones are held together with mortar as the faithful are linked by the bond of love ...[44]

The relationship of stone and Deity resonates through the Jewish liturgy where Deity is continually referred to in terms such as This is my God, I shall not fall, my Rock I grasp in troubled times, Rock of Ages, Rock of Israel, Rock of our life, Rock of our shelter, Rock of all ages, my Rock in whom there is no wrong, my Rock and my Redeemer, our Rock, and our Rock, the Rock of our Salvation.

> For in time of trouble, he shall hide me in his pavilion: in the secret of his tabernacle shall he hide me: he shall set me up upon a rock.
>
> Psalm 27: 5

A spiritual emphasizing God as being a refuge in the form of a rock is *I've got a Home in the Rock*. Augustus Toplady's stirring hymn, *Rock of Ages* is a fitting example of the power of stone and its function as a spiritual refuge:

> Rock of Ages, cleft for me,
> Let me hide myself in Thee …
> While I draw this fleeting breath,
> When mine eyes shall close in death,
> When I soar to worlds unknown,
> See Thee on Thy judgment throne,
> Rock of Ages, cleft for me,
> Let me hide myself in Thee.

The frequent rejection of religious truth is symbolized by the rejected stone in Psalm 118 and is quoted in Matthew and Luke. The cornerstone is now understood to refer to the keystone of the arch. The keystone of the arch was a symbol to the Jews of the completion of their faith gained by practicing the precepts of their religion. To Christians, the keystone was the symbol of Jesus fulfilling the prophecies of the Old Testament. The keystone was not simply a stone holding an arch together, but rather the fulfillment of religious belief and prophecy. When the rejected stone was rediscovered and used for its symbolic purpose, it would symbolize the glorious epiphany.

> The stone which the builders refused has become the headstone of the corner.
>
> Psalm 118: 22
>
> Jesus saieth unto them, did ye never read in the Scriptures, The stone which the builders rejected, the same is become the head of the corner: this is the Lord's doing and it is marvelous in our eyes?
>
> Matthew 21: 42

And he beheld them and said, What is this then that is written, The stone which the builders rejected, the same is become the head of the corner?

Luke 20: 17

If it so be, ye have tasted that the Lord is gracious. To whom coming, as unto a living stone ... Ye also, as lively stones, are built up a spiritual house, an holy priesthood, to offer up spiritual sacrifices, acceptable to God by Jesus Christ ... Behold, I lay in Sion a chief corner stone, elect, precious: and he that believeth on him shall not be confounded ... the stone which the builders disallowed, the same is made the head of the corner.

I Peter 2: 3–7

Jacob, in Genesis 28, on the road to Haran lay down to sleep using stones for his pillow. In his dream, he saw a ladder reaching from the earth to the heavens with angels of God ascending and descending on it. In this dream, God revealed to Jacob the future of the Jewish people. When Jacob awoke, he recognized that this place was the House of God and the Gate of Heaven, "And this stone which I have set for a pillar shall be God's House."[45] Jacob named the site of his dream Bethel, which in Hebrew means House of God. He then piled up the stones on which he had slept creating a pillar and poured oil on top of them. The stones were a memorial which symbolized Jacob's covenant with God and they were anointed just as were the Kings and High Priests of Israel.

The stone upon which Jacob slept was a sacred stone and a communication between heaven and earth as witnessed by the angels on the ladder in his dream. Jacob's Bethel was also an *omphalos*.[46] The mystical and sacred site which was regarded as the navel or center of the earth was called the *omphalos* of Delphi by the ancient Greeks and was believed by them to be a white stone beneath which was the center of the earth. It was the home of *Pytho*, the sacred serpent of Delphi. At this shrine, Apollo killed *Pytho*, and so the stone was a hierophany.[47] According to Pindar, as the center of the earth, the omphalos linked the dead who existed in the lower world, the living in the terrestrial world, and of the gods in heaven. It was the center of worship of Apollo and Plato wrote that Apollo had his center at this shrine at the world's center and navel, to guide mankind. The *omphalos* at Delphi also symbolized the life force which controlled the violent irrational powers of *Chaos*.[48]

The Temple Mount in Jerusalem, where the sacrifice of Isaac occurred, the Temple of Solomon later stood, and where the Dome of the Rock Mosque is now located, was also an *omphalos*. Hebrew legend states that the first stone used in building the world was laid here. In Genesis 1: 2, we read "And the earth was without form and void and darkness was upon the face of the deep." In Hebrew, the word for the deep is *tehom* which means the great deep of the primordial waters of creation. According to the Hebrew *Mishna*, the great Rock of the Temple in Jerusalem went down to the waters of the *Tehom* and covered the mouth of the *Tehom* creating the conjunction of the lower world and the terrestrial world.[49] The great rock and the Temple similarly formed an omphalos. The stone of Jacob's dream was also an *axis mundi*, the axis of the world, with the stone being the locus of the connection from the primordial waters of the underworld upward to earth at Jacob's stone and then continuing upward to heaven via Jacob's ladder.

The site where Jacob had his dream was referred to in Latin as *Baetulus* after the place name, Bethel, and baetylic stone is a general term describing a stone which is the habitation of deity. Baetylic stones were especially worshipped by the pre-Islamic Arabs as manifestations of the divine presence. This concept also spread throughout North Africa. These stones tended to become objects of direct image worship rather than being regarded as manifestations of divine action and as there were biblical injunctions against the actual worshipping of stones, these stones often had to be destroyed.[50]

> Ye shall make you no idols nor graven image, neither rear you up a standing image, neither shall you set up any image of stone in your land, to bow down unto it: for I am the Lord your God.
>
> Leviticus 26: 1

Bethel, the House or Dwelling Place of God, eventually became Bethlehem, which means the House of Bread in Hebrew. Stone thus became transmuted into a spiritual food. The symbolic presence of God at Bethel was changed to God as spiritual nourishment. Bread in the Eucharist undergoes an analogous transformation. Satan even tried to tempt Jesus to transform stones into bread:

> And when the tempter came to him, he said, If thou be the Son of God, command that these stones be made bread.
>
> Matthew 4: 3

Stone was considered to have a life force in the Bible, not only in its relationship to the spiritual bread, but by also by the ability to provide both water and honey. When Moses struck the stone in the desert, water gushed forth (Exodus 17: 6). In another passage, rock gives forth honey:

He should have fed them also with the finest of the wheat: and with honey out of the rock should I have satisfied thee.

Psalm 81: 16

Jacob was not alone in the Bible in using stones as a memorial to God. Joshua, after crossing the Jordan River, was commanded by God to set twelve stones in the river, where the priests stood while carrying the Ark of the Covenant, as a memorial to their covenant (Joshua 4: 3–24). Just before his death, Joshua set a great stone under a tree in Shechem as a witness to a covenant made that day between the Jewish people and God:

Behold, this stone shall be a witness unto us; for it hath heard all the words of the Lord which he spake unto us;

Joshua 24: 25–27

In the Bible, God is also described as being not only a rock but the rock that begat man. In the Book of Deuteronomy, there is the beautiful Song of Moses which Moses communicated to the people of Israel just before his death. It contains numerous references to the hierophany of rock:

He is the Rock, his work is perfect:

Deuteronomy 32: 4

He made him to suck honey out of the rock and oil out of the flinty rock.

Deuteronomy 32: 4

But Jeshurun waxed fat, and kicked: ... then he forsook God which made him, and lightly esteemed the Rock of his salvation.

Deuteronomy 32: 15

Of the Rock that begat thee thou art unmindful, and hast forgotten God that formed thee.

Deuteronomy 32: 18

In the Song of Moses, other gods are also given the description of a rock:

For their rock is not as our Rock,

Deuteronomy 32: 31

And he shall say, where are their gods, their rock in whom they trusted,

Deuteronomy 32: 37

So great and divine was the power of stone that early Hebrew tradition even forbade the Jews from using tools to shape stone. To artificially shape stone with tools would be to desacralize the work of God.[51] To the Jews, stone was an aniconic representation of the image of God, and to use tools on the image of God would be a desecration:

> And if thou wilt make me an altar of stone, thou shalt not build it of hewn stone: for if thou lift up thy tool upon it thou hast polluted it.
> Exodus 20: 25

Joshua built an altar to God on Mount Ebel which consisted of uncut stones on which no tools had been used, in accordance with the Law of Moses. Throughout biblical history, the Jews continued to build altars of unhewn stones.

Finally, when Solomon began to build the great Temple, it was apparent that uncut stones could no longer be used due to the size and complexity of the building. However in keeping with the spirit of the Mosaic injunctions against the use of tools to shape stone, the blocks of stone had to be cut and shaped in a place away from the Temple:

> And the house, when did was in building, was built of stone made ready before it was brought thither: so that there was neither hammer nor axe nor any tool of iron heard in the house, while it was in building.
> I Kings 6: 7

As the ancient Hebrews had become a settled people, the use of hewn stone instead of uncut stone had become allowable. In order to comply with the Biblical injunctions against using tools to cut stone, there was an ancient Hebrew legend that the perfect cutting and shaping of the stones for the Temple was done by a magical worm, called the *Shamir*, which functioned in a manner similar to that of an industrial laser. This ability of the *Shamir* resulted in the beautifully cut and shaped stones of the Temple of Solomon.

Westcott, refers to a manuscript of a Masonic Ritual of 1780 given to him by the Rev. A. S. A. Woodford. In the lecture on King Solomon's Temple in this ritual, the following sequence occurs:

> Question: What was the real secret our Grand Master H. A. B. was slain for not revealing?
> Answer: Not the S ... T ... and W ... of a Master Mason as is erroneously asserted but the wonderful properties of the noble insect, the s ... a [Shamir] which cut and shaped all the sacred utensils and holy vessels in King Solomon's Temple and also that famous stone called A ... sh ... o, that is held in such great veneration among ancient Freemasons.

The manuscript the goes on to describe how Hiram Abiff had a vault or room built beneath the Sanctum Sanctorum, twenty cubits in depth from the surface with a height equal to the height of the Holy of Holies, and in this vault he placed a wonderful cubic stone altar called A ... sh ... o, made of porphyry that had been cut, formed, and polished by the Shamir. The Shamir, a wonderful insect had been found by King Solomon and the legend was then related. Only Solomon, King of Israel, Hiram, King of Tyre, and Hiram Abiff knew in what position to place the insect on a stone so that it would be able to cut and polish it. The secret of this was later allegedly preserved among the ancient records in the hollow of the two great pillars of the Temple.

The manuscript further states that when, according to Masonic tradition, the three assassins killed Hiram Abiff, their reason for doing so was to learn the secret of the Shamir. The 1780 ritual goes on to state that the Shamir is sometimes called an insect and sometimes a worm. Westcott notes that, in addition to the Shamir which could allegedly cut and break stones, ancient lore revealed that a bird called the hoopoe could perform this action as well as a plant called the saxifrage. It was Westcott's feeling that in order for Freemasonry to be respected for its beautiful and profound teachings, its fraternal love, and its benevolence, Freemasonry had to abandon the story of the marvelous Shamir and adopt a more conventional approach to the cutting and shaping of stone.[52]

In Revelation, there is another mystical concept of a white stone possessing a mystical knowledge:

> He that hath an ear, let him hear what the Spirit saith unto the churches; To him that overcometh will I give to eat of the hidden manna, and will give him a white stone and in the stone a new name written, which no man knoweth saving he that receiveth it.
>
> Revelation 2: 17

Jesus is also specifically referred to as a spiritual Rock:

> And did all drink the same spiritual drink: for they drank of that spiritual Rock that followed them: and that rock was Christ.
>
> I Corinthians 10: 4

On the sarcophagus of Junius Bassus (d.358), a divine lamb is shown striking a rock from which pours a stream of water. As the lamb is a symbol of Jesus, this scene links Jesus with Moses and the spiritual rock from which issued forth the spiritual water.[53] Another early use of the rock in Christian symbolism was to show a rock with four streams of water flowing from it representing the four Gospels that flowed forth from Deity.[54] These four flowing streams of the Gospels were analogous to the four rivers that flowed out of the Garden of Eden, Pison, Gihon, Hiddekel, and Euphrates. Bernardo Fungal, about 1500, painted St. Clement also striking a massive stone with his mattock. The water was shown flowing out of the rock for the Christian workers in a quarry symbolized their spiritual nourishment which was provided by the rock.

In more modern times, on the fourth mission to the moon, astronaut Jim Irwin picked up the Genesis Rock, a 4.15 billion year-old piece of primordial crust and insisted that at that moment, he heard the voice of God. Irwin was later to found a ministry.[55]

TALKING STONES

Another characteristic of stone was the ability of certain stones in Mesoamerica to have to have the power of speech. According to the *Anales de Xahil*, obsidian was a talking stone with the power of speech and may have referred to an oracle. This black stone was deified and was considered to be the heart of the earth.[56] There are references to talking statues dating back to the beginnings of literature. The legendary oracle at Delphi was but one example. The seventeenth-century Jesuit scholars Athanasius Kircher and Gregorio de Sepibus wrote about talking statuary in antiquity and how they considered these to be fraudulent. Miguel de Cervantes, the author of *Don Quixote*, also depicted the bewildered Don Quixote deceived by a fraudulent statue of a talking enchanted head.[57] There were prior sources of the artificial oracular devices and even St. Thomas Aquinas referred to them as not being theologically dangerous as he considered them to be frivolous.[58]

An early example of a talking stone statue is found in the third century B.C.E. Alexandrian poet Callimachus' *Book of Iambi*. Iamb IX features a talking ithyphallic statue which was actually the god Hermes, who in explaining the physical form which he had taken, attributed his obvious state of sexual arousal to a mystery rather than to lust.[59] In medieval Wales, there was a legend that when a corpse bound for interment in the cemetery was carried over Lechlevar, which was a large stone spanning the river Alun which lay between the church and the cemetery, the marble stone would break into speech. This caused it to crack in the middle and the fissure is still visible.[60]

Pasquino was the name given to an ancient stone statue unearthed in Rome during road construction work and which was placed in a small square near the

Piazza Navona in 1501. This statue was given the vicarious power of speech as people who wished to criticize the Pope or individuals in his government could express their dissatisfaction by writing satirical poems, called *pasquinades*, on posters and attaching them late at night to the statue thus making it a talking statue. Soon, there were numerous other talking statues in Rome.[61] They served a purpose similar to today's blogs or radio call-in talk shows.

STONE IN THE VISUAL ARTS

A further appreciation of the spiritual nature of stone can be gained by analyzing the role that stone plays in art. Rock formations and mountains have long attracted and fascinated artists and rocks can serve as artistic icons on their own. Chinese scholars long appreciated the spirituality of stone and would keep "spirit stones" in their libraries and gardens as they felt that these stones contained spiritual qualities and represented the forces of nature. These stones were displayed for contemplation and a sizable artistic and literary genre existed devoted to rocks and to rock collecting. The abstract formal qualities of unusual stones appealed to these scholars who felt that rocks simulated mountains, animals, or the grandeur of nature. Wooden stands for displaying the rocks were widespread in the Ming Dynasty and the displayed rocks were appreciated similar to today's antiques.[62]

The great hanging scrolls of China and Japan also used mountains of giant rocks as a recurring motifs that emphasized the power and grandeur of nature. One's eyes are led upward from tiny images of people and villages to large overpowering mountains of giant rocks that sweep upward to merge with and dissolve into the mists. The power of the giant rock formations that form the mountains, compared to the tiny depictions of people in these scrolls, stresses the insignificance of man in nature in comparison to the grandeur of the rocks. The rocks that form the soaring mountains in these paintings are manifestations of the cosmic mountain linking heaven and earth. This is the cosmic bridge or link between the world of the profane and the world of the sacred. Symbolically, the top of the cosmic mountain was an *omphalos*.

Stone has always inspired artists. Leonardo da Vinci created three paintings called the Virgin or the Madonna of the Rocks. One is in the National Gallery in London, another is in the Louvre, and a third is in the Chéramy collection in Switzerland. Mary is shown in a grotto bringing the infants Jesus and John the Baptist together while on the flight to Egypt. The individual figures are overshadowed by the massive rocks of the grotto.

There is a recognition that stone can be shaped by the sculptor to relate the inner feelings, the passions, and the subconscious of man. As Percy Bysshe Shelley wrote in Ozymandius in 1818:

> I met a traveler from an antique land
> Who said: Two vast and trunkless legs of stone
> Stand in the desert ... Near them, on the sand,
> Half sunk, a shattered visage lies, whose frown,
> And wrinkled lip, and sneer of cold command,
> Tell that its sculptor well those passions read
> Which yet survive, stampd on these lifeless things,
> The hand that mocked them, and the heart that fed;
> And on the pedestal these words appear:
> 'My name is Ozymandius, king of kings:
> Look on my works, ye Mighty, and despair!'
> Nothing beside remains. Round the decay
> Of that colossal wreck, boundless and bare
> The lone and level sands stretch far away.

Vasari related that one day Michelangelo was found working on an imperfect piece of black marble. When asked why he spent his time sculpting this imperfect stone, Michelangelo was said to have replied, "I am releasing the angel within."

It was necessary to release the living creature from the outer husk of stone that enclosed them. Michelangelo's poetry describes his stony lover, a person of adamantine hardness, who was the only one whom Michelangelo felt could release him from the outer shell concealing him. Michelangelo's sculptural hardness of his female muse that resonated throughout his poetry found echoes in literature, such as Keats *La Belle Dame Sans Merci*.

Goethe in a sonnet of 1807–08 compared the coldness of the stone woman to that of actual stone:

> Like it, no sign of life thou giv'st to me;
> Compared with thee, the stone appears to glow.[63]

In Michelangelo's poem No. 152, he describes the living soul in "hard and alpine stone" and that by removing this stone, the living figure contained within would grow larger, i.e. emerge. In referring to the good deeds in his soul, only his lover could remove them from the coarse and crude outer husk:

You alone can take them out
From within my outer shell, ...[64]

As a poet, Michelangelo wrote more than eighty sonnets as well as hundreds of other types of poems. To Michelangelo, stone had an inner illumination that waited for the sculptor to bring it out.

Not even the best of artists has any conception that a single marble block does not contain
Within its excess, and *that* is only attained by the hand that obeys the intel-lect.[65]

To Michelangelo, stone was a living force upon which he worked. His role was to reveal the life within the stone. This was the concept of *pietra viva* or living stone, a widespread concept in Italian culture. The capturing of life in stone was a transformation type of mystery. Variations of this included Pygmalion's creating a woman in ivory so beautiful that she was brought to life or Medusa's turning people who gazed at her into stone.[66] Michelangelo expressed thoughts similar to Pygmalion:

I believe I could, even were you made of stone, love you so faithfully that I'd be able
To make you come with me at more than a walk;[67]

The vitality of stone was on ongoing characteristic of Michelangelo's work with divine power as only one of the attributes of stone. In his early St. Peter's *Pietà*, stone becomes Michelangelo's expression of divinity in which the peaceful beauty of the Virgin's face as she holds her son on her lap serves as a visual metaphor of a sacred and celestial mystery as her face is cold and hard without any trace of emotion. Mary appears no older than her son as she cradles the virtually naked Jesus in her lap. At the time of its completion, there were complaints of having Mary appear to be the same age as her son and appearing as a fully dressed young woman holding this undressed young man on her lap. Since the twelfth century, Mary had been identified as the 'bride' of Christ as well as the beloved of the Song of Songs. This was however the first time that this role was seen in a *Pietà*. Apparently, there was a considerable shock at seeing the Virgin and Christ displayed in this manner, as two young beautiful people or even lovers with the stone woman image of the greater than life-size Virgin.[68]

The emotional detachment seen in the stoniness of the Virgin's face recurs in his various Madonnas in contrast to the violent contortions, emotion, and power exuded in the slave series. As a counterpoint to the cold beauty of her face in the St. Peter's *Pietà*, the wide billowing folds of the dress on her lap as she supports Jesus are massive, with a deep V formed by the drapery across her spread knees, adding a powerful strength and solidity to the Virgin. Strength, beauty, and a deep inner wisdom recur continually as a theme throughout Michelangelo's art adding further dimensionality to the symbolic meaning of stone.

Whether it be the insightful and perceptive stare of the gigantic statue of David in the Galleria dell'Accademia in Florence, the penetrating gaze of his statue of Moses in San Pietro in Vincoli church in Rome, or the thoughtful Lorenzo de' Medici statue in the Medici Tombs in Florence, Michelangelo imparted a magical quality to stone transforming it into a seemingly living being. Even the dead Jesus in the St. Peter's *Pietà* seems vibrantly alive. In Michelangelo's hands, the symbolic religious iconography which is stone becomes suddenly a living entity.

Michelangelo's sculptural hardness of his female muse that resonated throughout his poetry found numerous antecedents and echoes throughout the literary world. Dante Alighieri, who whose poetry Michelangelo adored and whom he frequently read and quoted, wrote four poems called the *rime petrose* about his anguish over his unrequited love for an unidentified lady. In each of these, this lady is compared to a stone in terms of her coldness and cruelty towards him. She is the *donna petra* or *donna petrosa*, the mysterious woman of stone.

> She was more cruelty than she was woman …
> Thus with her face, that is forever cold,
> She freezes this my blood at any time,

There is however, an inward loveliness as this cold and cruel woman is redeemed in his eyes via her special communication to Dante:

> She is the harbour of all beauty's light …
> That I see splendour even in the stone …
> 'Tis from her eyes sweet light descends to me.

Yet, Dante reflects on her growing harshness:

> I want to change my words with so much harshness
> As this enchanting stone has in her actions[69]

In the Italian Renaissance poem O cessate di piagarmi *(Oh, Leave me to Die)* by Nicola Minato and set to music by Alessandro Scarlatti, the lady of stone and ice is told

> *O cessate di piagarmi,*
> *o lasciatemi morir! ...*
> *Più del gelo e più de' marmi*
> *fredde e sorde a' miei martir.*
>
> O stop wounding me,
> o leave me to die! ...
> more than ice and more than marble
> cold and deaf to my sufferings![70]

A frequently recurring theme in Renaissance poetry is the concept of dying in the arms of the beloved woman of stone. This act of dying in the cold lover's arms was a euphemism for orgasm and there is a parallel of this sexual allusion with stone's long use as a fertility icon.

> Even as she kills me ...
> She promises me all my joys[71]

The stony woman is however not inevitably an adored object and the stoniness can have other connotations. In Book 4–2 of Dickens' Our Mutual Friend, we read:

> and then Ma came to see, oh such a dreadful old stony woman from the country ...[72]

STONE IN PREHISTORIC ART

Stone has also served as a medium for artists to use for painting for many thousands of years and probably served as the first canvas. There are about 350 to 400.000 rock art sites scattered around the world and the number of images is probably in the tens of millions. Africa alone has more than 100,000 and possibly as many as 200,000 sites. In addition to paintings, there are sculptures and engravings on stone.[73]

Stone has been used for the abstract human and animal forms seen in the Paleolithic drawings and paintings from the great caves of Spain and France such as

Altamira, Lascaux, Les Trois Frères, Chauvet, and Cosquer. One can only imagine the possible scene of the young male initiates of the tribe being led down to these underground caves, crawling in the deep darkness in their initiatic ceremonies, to enter into a vast underground cavern in which they were confronted with blazing torches and flickering oil lamps confronting a whole panoply of human and beautiful and powerful animal figures painted on the stone walls. The Paleolithic artists developed techniques that took western civilization thousands of years to discover. One of the great technological achievements of these people was an understanding of perspective as shown in the bison in the Lascaux cave. This intricate mastery of perspective was not seen again in European art until thousands of years later in the works of the 13th century master, Paolo Uccelli.[74]

We have no written records from Paleolithic times but there seems to have been a certain ritualistic element in these great rich and complex paintings on stone found in the caves of Spain and France, which appeared about 32,000 years ago and lasted for 20,000 years with relatively little change in overall format. Certain animals such as horses, bison, and reindeer and certain geometric signs appear again and again in the Franco-Cantabrian cave paintings. Fish, insects, rodents, reptiles, and mammals such as hyenas, were virtually never painted and there must have been other strict conventions about things not to be painted such as the sun, moon, stars, trees, flowers, and natural landmarks such as rivers, cliffs, rocks, and caves. Animals and people were never shown mating. Even the artistic techniques and the color scheme remained the same during this more than 20,000 year period. These animals, painted on stone, would have had a very specific place as well as a ritual significance in the culture of these people.

This was an ongoing Franco-Cantabrian cultural tradition and civilization lasting more than 20,000 years, spreading over hundreds of miles from Northern Spain across the Pyrenees into Southern France, and was passed on through hundreds generation long before the invention of writing. This was truly a prehistoric school of art which would have involved not only the teaching of the concepts of knowledge and beliefs but also the skills of painting.[75] The caves with their iconic animals on the rock walls were the repository of the culture of this otherwise lost civilization. On these beautifully painted rock walls are the symbols of the history and the unchanging religious faith of a people. One can only wonder as to how many sites are lost to us as cave entrances collapsed or were buried in landslides or earthquakes. For this art to have been preserved over 20,000 years, there must have been an extensive series of caves that were worked on which have been lost to us.

According to Abbé Breuil, the pre-eminent 19th century figure in prehistory, the work of the cave artists was a "collective social affair, showing a true spiritual unity...."[76] There must have been an incredible communal effort to produce this art. Not only were artists necessary but also assistants to bring the paints, food and other supplies that the artists needed in the caves. People were necessary to drag tree trunks down into the caves to create scaffolds as many of the paintings were many meters above the cave floors. Others were necessary to tend the lamps that would have had to be lit to illuminate the deep darkness of the caves. The spiritual unity involved would have involved an extensive network of communications between these various groups, not only geographic but also spanning 20 millennia. Lacking the written word and with only the most basic forms of communication, this remarkable civilization still endured. We can only surmise how it functioned, but the rites conducted in these prehistoric caves would have been accompanied by music as flutes and whistles were also found in the caves. Elders would have been needed to teach the tenets of this remarkable civilization to ensuing generations.

What is also apparent was that these were not flat paintings on a flat surface but instead had a three dimensionality. The contours of animals were often painted over bulges in the rock walls and the artists would have searched out suitable areas of the walls. This would have meant that the animals were suggested by the rock walls rather than the artists imposing their own ideas on the surface.[77] The animals which were already within rock were being pulled out, similar to the Bound Captives of Michelangelo fighting to release themselves from stone some 12 to 35,000 years later. Animals were often painted so that they appeared to be emerging from crevices in the rock walls. This three-dimensionality gave an incredible vitality to the animals in these beautiful paintings.

The Paleolithic artists used the natural contours of the rock walls in their art which would have corresponded to a belief in supernatural forces dwelling inside the rock. In the rock art of various cultures, the exiting of animals from natural crevices in the rock walls, again demonstrated that rock was a dwelling place of supernatural beings. There was a very specific intrinsic relationship between the rock substrate and the figures painted upon it.

The tracing of isolated hands on the rock walls was also one of the most common motifs, not only in the Franco-Cantabrian Paleolithic caves, but was also almost universally seen, being found in rock paintings throughout the world including among others, Armenia, Borneo, Australia, Arizona, Utah, California, and Argentina. The Cueva de las Manos in Argentina was used for 8,000 years and thousands of hand stencils were probably made. About 830 of these still exist. These handprints were made by coating the hand with paint and then pressing the hand against the rock wall. This may have been a means of communication among hunters or part of some unknown religious ritual.[78]Among the American Indians, the handprint on rock was a signature so that the gods would know who had made the supplications.[79]Another technique of creating the outline of a hand on rock would have been to blow paint over one's hand which was pressed against the rock, thereby binding the hand and by extension the person, to the underlying rock as a mystical communion.

Another recurring motif was the use of small cupules or cavities. These were cut into the rock and measured a couple of centimeters wide. These cupules have been found in all the inhabited continents and date back to the Neanderthal tomb at La Ferrassie. These cupules may have served a functional purpose such as scraping a rock to get powder. There is also a female sexual connotation as they have been shown to be associated with vulvas which were another frequently recurring symbol in rock art. Among the Hokan Indians of northern California, cupules were made as part of a fertility ritual. Before intercourse, the powder from the hollowed out cupule would be placed on or in the woman's body as a cure for sterility. In Australia, the cupules were used to assist the procreation of favored birds. Elsewhere in California, the creation of cupules was used to bring about rain or wind.[80]

The power of stone thus exerted its powerful hierophanic presence in art and primitive society long before we could ever conceive of schools of art as having existed.

STONE ELSEWHERE IN LITERATURE

The symbolic beauty, power, and the ability to transmute both to and from stone are found throughout literature. In Greek mythology, Niobe angered Leto, the mother of Apollo and Artemis. Niobe's children were then killed and Niobe fled to Asia Minor where Zeus turned her into a stone statue that wept perpetually. Shakespeare's Hamlet described his mother's behavior at his father's funeral as, "Like Niobe, all tears." In Christopher Marlowe's Dido, Queen of Carthage, Niobe is turned into stone.

> O my Achates, Theban Niobe,
> Who for her sons' death wept out life and breath
> And, dry with grief, was turned into a stone …

O, yet this stone doth make Aeneas weep!
And would my prayers (as Pygmalion's did)
Could give it life[81]

A somewhat different variation of the transformation to stone was the story of Iphis and Anaxarte. Ovid in the Metamorphoses tells the tale of a youth Iphis who fell passionately in love with the beautiful young woman Anaxarte. Anaxarte cruelly and harshly spurned his love and finally, out of desperation, Iphis killed himself. Even Iphis' death did not change move Anaxarte and Aphrodite punished her by turning her into stone. [82]

Other transmutations into and from stone are found in Spenser's, The Faery Queen.

No magicke arts hereof had any might,
Nor bloudie wordes of bold Enchaunters call,
But all that was not such, as seemd in sight,
Before that shield did fade, and suddeine fall:
And when him list the raskall routes appall,
Men into stones therewith he could transmew,
And stones to dust, and dust to nought at all;
And when him list the prouder lookes subdew,
He would them gazing blind, or turne to other hew.[83]

She set her downe to weepe for sore constraint,
And to Diana calling lowd for ayde,
Her deare besought, to let her dye a mayd.
The goddesse heard, and suddeine where she sate,
Welling out streames of teares, and quite dismayd
With stony feare of that rude rustick mate,
Transformd her to a stone from stedfast virgins state.[84]

The metaphysical power of stone as a force of protection was also described by Christopher Marlowe in his epic poem, Tamburlaine The Great.

An ointment which a cunning alchymist
Distilled from the purest balsamum
And simplest extracts of all minerals,
In which the essential form of marble stone,
Temper'd by science metaphysical,
And spells of magic from the mouths of spirits,
With which if you but 'noint your tender skin,
Nor pistol, sword, nor lance, can pierce your flesh.[85]

Stone was also used symbolically to describe the majesty and beauty of England in Shakespeare's *King Richard II*, Act 2, Scene 1:

> This precious stone set in the silver sea ...
> This blessed plot, this earth, this realm, this England.

In Shakespeare's *As You Like It*, Act 2, Scene 1, the speaking power of stone is again stated this time as sermons in stone:

> And this our life exempt from publike haunt,
> Findes tongues in trees, bookes in the running brookes,
> Sermons in stones, and good in euery thing

As a way to express the power, majesty and eternity of stone as a counterpoint to mankind's inherent weakness, Lamar Herrin uses the commentary of the ever-practical Sancho Panza in Cervantes' *Don Quixote*.

> I was right, the Sancho Panza in me was right. Better to worship the stone. If you're looking for a way to escape the terms of your trifling existence, better to put yourself in touch with geological history, where you're nothing, an infinitesimal instant in the ageless uplift of mountains and the ageless grinding of them down. Put your hand on a cliff face if you want to get right your place in the chronicle of time. You're an overnight, crevice-growing weed, nothing more. But you have your moment in the crevice. Bolstered, protected, nurtured by stone, you and your fellow weeds can take a certain comfort in that. It's a community of sorts.
> Sancho Panza would have said, But Master, my good Don Quixote. Look at that stone and look at us. The stone stands. We're so weak that every few hours we have to lie down. It's as plain as day, *como una catedral de claro*. Why all that fuss?
> But my Sancho Panza lies asleep.[86]

Another expression of the mystery of stone is contained in Charles Simic's poem Stone where there is just enough light so that one can enter into the stone discovering its mystical interior:

> Go inside a stone
> That would be my way.
> ...
> Just enough light to make out
> The strange writings, the star-charts

On the inner walls. [87]

Another aspect of stone as a living entity was described by Thomas Babbington Macaulay in The Prophecy of Capys in *Lays of Ancient Rome* where Capys prophesizes to Romulus of the future defeat of the Greeks by the Romans:

> The stone that breathes and struggles,
> The brass that seems to speak;—
> Such cunning they who dwell on high
> Have given unto the Greek.[88]

Stone is also involved in metaphors of the death process. There is finality to stone and a presentiment of unknown horrors. T.S. Eliot's poem, *The Hollow Men*, presents a particularly harrowing image of death with stone figuring prominently in the imagery. The hollow men are those who crossed to death's other kingdom where stone images are raised. In this land of death, the

> Lips that would kiss
> Form prayers to broken stone. [89]

The power of stone is however challenged by William Shakespeare in his 65th Sonnet in which he shows physical things, even including stone, cannot withstand the power of the "wreckful siege of the battering days." It is only the power of the written word that can preserve beauty of his lover against the ravages of time.

> Since brass, nor stone, nor earth, nor boundless sea,
> But sad mortality o'ersways their power,
> How with this rage shall beauty hold a plea,
> Whose action is no stronger than a flower?
> O! how shall summer's honey breath hold out,
> Against the wrackful siege of battering days,
> When rocks impregnable are not so stout,
> Nor gates of steel so strong but Time decays?
> O fearful meditation! where, alack,
> Shall Time's best jewel from Time's chest lie hid?
> Or what strong hand can hold his swift foot back?
> Or who his spoil of beauty can forbid?
> O! none, unless this miracle have might,
> That in black ink my love may still shine bright.

Freemasonry figured prominently in two of the most challenging books to be found in literature, James Joyce's *Ulysses* and *Finnegans Wake* which contain hundreds of allusions to Freemasonry. Joyce was not a mason but had intensively researched the subject. *Ulysses* and *Finnegans Wake* not only contain references to the first three degrees of Freemasonry, but to Royal Arch Masonry and other orders within the Craft as well. Included in *Finnegans Wake* is a part of the Obligation of the Entered Apprentice Degree.[90] Other references scattered throughout Joyce's *Finnegans Wake* and *Ulysses* which will be readily appreciated by Freemasons include:

> A white lambskin peeps out of his waistcoat pocket …[91]

> this new book of Morses responded most remarkably to the silent query of the world's oldest light … it was pierced but punctured by numerous stabs and foliated gashes made with a pronged instrument.[92]

Finnegans Wake also contains reference to the transformative powers involving stone within Freemasonry. There is a paraphrasing of the Masonic ritual of tyling or securing the lodge in order to open the lodge and bring light to the Craft and subsequently to close the lodge. The following sequence referring to the activities of the Inner Guard and the Tyler (Outer Guard) who tyle the lodge in British Freemasonry (in American Freemasonry, the Tyler and the Junior Deacon perform these duties):

> Thou hast closed the portals of the habitations of thy children and thou hast set the guards, thereby, even Garda Didymus and Garda Domas, that thy children may read in the book of the opening of the mind to light and err not in the darkness …[93]

Didymus means twin and Domas refers to Thomas. In the non-canonical *Acts of Thomas,* Judas Thomas is said to be the twin of Jesus. The parallel of Jesus and Thomas (Didymus and Domas) in this part of the Masonic ritual consists of the twin officers, the Inner Guard and the Tyler (Outer Guard), closing the lodge doors thereby tyling or securing the lodge. Thus begins the ritual of the Lodge opening which leads to bringing the light of Deity into the Lodge by opening the Volume of the Sacred Law (in western lands, the Bible). This is means by which the Initiate is brought from darkness to light. The above passage from *Finnegans Wake* is followed by these cryptic lines derived from the *Bearlagair Na Sair,* the "secret language" of Freemasons allegedly used in certain counties of Ireland, which refers to the bonds of Freemasonry among Masonic Brothers.[94] The twinning of tree and stone by Joyce which immediately follows, again parallels the two "Twins", Jesus and Thomas and the bonding of Brothers.

> Till tree from tree, tree among trees, tree over tree become stone to stone, stone between stones, stone under stone forever ...[95]

THE POWER OF STONE IN THEATRE AND MUSIC: THE LEGEND OF DON JUAN/DON GIOVANNI

In music and theatre, there are some major expressions of the hierophany of stone. In Giuseppe Verdi's majestic opera, Aida, Rhadames, the Egyptian general and war hero has been condemned to death for inadvertently revealing the battle plans of the Egyptian army to the enemy Ethiopian General Amonasro who is the father of his beloved Aida. Rhadames is condemned to die by being entombed alive for his moral sin against not only his country, but the gods. As the stone of entombment is lowered into place, he sings 'La fatal pietra sovra me si chiuse ... Ecco la tomba mia.'[96] The fatal stone has closed upon me ... Here is my tomb. Stone again serves as the hierophanic agent for punishing moral sins.

However, the most powerful example of the hierophany of stone in opera is based on the legendary story of Don Juan, or in Italian, Don Giovanni. Here, a triple hierophany of stone occurs, viz., a stone statue transmuted to a stone person with divine powers, stone as the vehicle for repentance and salvation, and lastly, stone as the vehicle for divine retribution. The hierophanic powers of stone eventually become the climax of what is arguably the greatest opera ever written, Mozart's *Don Giovanni*.

This story of the death of the legendary Don Juan was so powerful that in the three and a half centuries since the Spanish monk, Tirso de Molina, wrote the first recorded Don Juan drama, *El Burlador de Sevilla y Convidado de Piedra*, (The Seducer or Trickster of Seville and the Stone Guest) about 1630, hundreds of playwrights, poets and composers have taken the story of the legendary libertine with its powerful death scene as their subject. Tirso de Molina' story of Don Juan Tenorio was based on medieval legends, and was followed by Moliere's *Dom Juan ou le Festin de Pierre* in 1665. E. T. A. Hofmann's short story, *Don Juan*, published in 1813 was a fantasy which confronted two powerful and diametrically opposed forces, "the conflict between the divine and the demonic forces is the essence of earthly life."[97] George Bernard Shaw adopted Mozart's version of the story as Act III of his play *Man and Superman* and this act has been produced on the stage as a dramatic separate work entitled *Don Juan in Hell*.

The basic story line of the Don Juan genre generally consists of two parts. In the first, the notorious libertine, Don Juan, pursues numerous women with the intent of seducing them. In the second part, after killing the father of one of his former lovers in a duel, he encounters the stone statue of the dead father in a graveyard. Don Juan sarcastically invites the statue to have dinner with him and the stone statue, which is transmuted back to life, agrees. At the dinner, the stone statue offers Don Juan the chance to repent his sins, but Don Juan refuses. Denying the chance of salvation, the statue drags Don Juan down to his eternal damnation in Hell.

More than 40 operas are based on the Don Juan legend, including Alexander Dargomyzhsky's *Stone Guest* which was based on a poem by Pushkin who was a Freemason as was Mozart. This two-act opera, left unfinished at his death in 1869, was completed by Cesar Cui and orchestrated by Rimsky-Korsakov.[98] Franz Liszt set the story to music in the grandiose piano fantasia *Réminiscences de Don Juan*. Liszt's music was based on Mozart's version of *Don Giovanni*, but Liszt chose to begin *Réminiscences* with the awesome music of the somber encounter of Don Giovanni and the stone statue. Liszt's music focuses on the damnation of Don Juan with the amorous intrigues playing a secondary role. Mozart's delightful music of the first half of the opera is incorporated into Liszt's improvisations and is infused by Liszt with a sinister and menacing foreboding, losing its pastoral innocence. The manic Champagne aria, *Finch'han dal vino,* in which Don Giovanni looks forward to his licentious dinner, is transformed by Liszt's brilliance into a reminiscence of the powerful opening music of the damnation of Don Giovanni by the power of the stone guest. It is the salvation/damnation part of the legend that has now become paramount. The power of stone has become the major theme of the work. Not only Liszt, but Richard Strauss as well, composed music on this subject with his *Don Juan* in 1889.[99][100]

Pushkin's play, written in verse, was entitled the Stone Guest and Don Guan (Don Juan/Don Giovanni) was no longer the principal character but instead was secondary to the stone statue, known as the Commendatore, who dominated the play. Don Juan is again rendered powerless by the statue.[101] The theme of the choice of repentance/divine retribution versus eternal damnation by the hierophany of the power of the stone statue often dominated the intrigues in the Don Juan stories and music.

It is in the incredibly dramatic music of Mozart's *Don Giovanni* where the hierophanic power of stone is most powerfully presented. The real, but rarely used, title of Mozart's *Don Giovanni* is *Il Dissoluto Punito, ossia Don Giovanni*, which needs no translation. An emotional maelstrom is unleashed by the hierophanies of stone and a cosmic battle of salvation versus repentance is waged. In the chilling damnation finale, of Mozart's version, the stone statue of the Commendatore who has been transmuted back to life although still in the form of the stone statue is mockingly invited by Don Giovanni in the graveyard scene to come to dinner in his home. At the dinner, in a series of mounting, soul wrenching, ominous crescendos of terrifying and chilling D minor chords demanding Don Giovanni's repentance, Don Giovanni is pushed by the menacing, slowly but ever-advancing stone statue, towards the chasm between Heaven and Hell. Unlike Tirso's *El Burlador de Sevilla*, Mozart has the stone statue coming to first offer Don Giovanni salvation by repentance.[102] The statue invites Don Giovanni to dine with him at his own table where he eats the "celestial bread". "Repent!" is the command of the Commendatore. There is a thundering "No!" by Don Giovanni. Again, "Repent!" and again and yet again the thundering "No!" "There is no more time ..." says the statue. Don Giovanni has made his choice, eternal damnation.

The power of stone through its vehicle of the stone statue is an unstoppable force. The stone statue, coming from the land of the dead is not only a hierophany in the form of the vehicle of repentance and salvation for Don Giovanni but also serves the second hierophanic function as an avenging angel of God. Don Giovanni is man confronting his mortality as well as staring down the power of the universe. There is a tension and a dialectic between the ethical and the spiritual, and between the hierophany of repentance and salvation by the power of stone versus its ability to commit one to eternal damnation.

In this Faustian moment, defying God and man alike, the unrepentant Don Giovanni commits the ultimate defiance of God. Turning down the chance of salvation offered by the stone statue by refusing to repent and, similar to the collapse and destruction of a mighty burning edifice, Don Giovanni is engulfed in the abyss of Hell. Unflinching and unrepentant to the end, astride the chasm between the enlightenment and the romantic period in the violence of his defiance, Don Giovanni becomes the great romantic period hero; one with the Promethean inner strength to defy man, God, and the universe.

The virtually overwhelming power within the hierophanic stone statue, unleashed with its accompanying terrifying music in *Don Giovanni,* is engaged in a decisive battle; it is the power of the universe in its intimate connection with even the most restless, passion—ridden human existence.[103] These two powers coexist and yet are in an eternal cycle of conflict of life and death. Mozart's music complements and enhances the dramatic effect. Hermann Hesse described the beautiful and awful music of *Don Giovanni* at the moment of the entrance of the Commendatore:

> ... it rang through the ghostly house, coming from the other world, from the immortals. Mozart' I thought ... the most beloved and exalted picture that my inner life contained.[104]

Man can rage against nature as did King Lear but cannot hope to prevail against this immense and overwhelming force of nature representing both divine justice and divine love. As Kierkegaard wrote, No power on earth is able to defeat Don Juan; only a spirit, an apparition from another world can do that ...[105] It is only the all-powerful hierophany of stone that can attempt to conquer the Don. Stone, as hierophany, may have the strength of the universe behind it, but even the power of stone cannot fully subdue the unquenchable Don who will go to his eternal damnation fighting the power of the universe reflected in stone. There is a sense that despite his descent into Hell, Don Juan is still with us planning his next amorous intrigue. The hierophanic power of stone is still with us today as an overwhelming force on the operatic stage fighting the demonic powers resident in society.

THE SYMBOLISM OF STONE IN FREEMASONRY

The hierophanic aspect of stone also has a major role in Freemasonry. The emotional impact of stone is apparent in the Scottish Rite Entered Apprentice Degree at the very beginning of the candidate's journey. The Candidate enters a small room called the Chamber of Reflection, analogous to the cave where early man was initiated into the concepts of the Great Mystery. At the door of the Chamber of Reflection, the candidate is transported into a strange and mystical world. The visual cues of the normal outside modern rationalistic world are no longer present but are replaced with a whole set of new cues reflecting strange images and words. Infused with the pungent smell of incense, the Chamber of Reflection is dimly lit by a candle. The walls are black and on a small table at which the candidate sits, are a skull, crossed thigh bones, some bread, salt, sulfur, water, and an hour glass, which convey various symbolic meanings of which the candidate is not yet aware. Seated at the table, he is told to write his Last Will. Facing himself in a small mirror, the Candidate has the psychological imperative of having to directly confront himself in a silent self-examination. One cannot hide from oneself. On the walls of the Chamber are murals showing a scythe and a cockerel. Also inscribed in white letters on the black walls of the chamber are mysterious letters V.I.T.R.I.O.L. These letters refer to the Latin phrase *visita interiora, rectificando invenies occultam lapidum* which means, visit the center of the earth and by rectifying you shall find the hidden stone.[106] Stone is therefore among first Masonic symbols that the Candidate encounters with the message that in his Masonic journey, he too will visit the ends of the earth reflected in his journey of self-discovery in which he will search and uncover this hidden stone. Alone in the Chamber, the Candidate begins his focus on the mysteries of life and death in this, his first step in his Masonic journey. These are mysteries which he himself will visit and experience in his Masonic travel.

The special meaning of stone has long been held to be related to the soul and deity. In the First Degree, the new Mason is told that he is a spiritual cornerstone upon which he will erect his future moral and Masonic edifice.[107] He is also told that our minds are fitted as living stones for that spiritual building, eternal in the heavens.[108] In the First Degree, the initiate is introduced to the first of a series of working tools of the operative stone mason which he is taught hold rich and deep philosophical and religious import. He will use these mystical tools in his symbolic work with stone.

In an old Scottish ritual, the smooth stone or ashlar is said to represent the stone on which the angel with the flaming sword stood when he expelled Adam and Eve from the Garden of Eden. It also represents the altar where Abraham was about to sacrifice Isaac as well as the stone upon which Jacob laid his head when he had his famous dream.[109] In a 1722 French ritual, the concept of the living stones is found which is similar to the present Blue Lodge ritual.

> Ye are living stones, built up into a spiritual House, who believe and rely on the chief Lapis Angularis (the Cornerstone) which the refractory and disobedient Builders disallowed ...[110]

Every Masonic Lodge has two constant symbols, the rough and the smooth stones or ashlars. The new Entered Apprentice is told of the symbolic importance of using the mallet to remove the rough edges of the unhewn ashlar in order to prepare it for use by the more experienced craftsman. The transformation of the rough ashlar into the smooth ashlar, by means of the various symbolic tools received in each Degree, symbolizes the progression of the new Mason in his search for Masonic light.

The importance of squared stone is an ancient concept dating back to antiquity. In the 12th-13th century, Pierre de Roissy wrote of the spirituality of the stones in a church:

> Squared stones signify the squareness of the virtues of the saints ... The polished stones represent the saints polished by adversity.[111]

The presence of stone in the Lodge goes back to the early days of Freemasonry. In the Catechism in the *Edinburgh Register House* manuscript of 1696, as well as in the virtually identical *Chetwood Crawley* and the *Kevan* manuscripts from the same period, the earliest description of the Perpend Ashlar is found.

> Q. Are there any jewels in your lodge?
> A. Yes, three, Perpend Esler a Square pavement and a broad oval

The Perpend Esler or Ashlar is a dressed block of stone which is longer than it is wide or deep. A Perpend Ashlar could be a stone similar in shape to two stone cubes joined together so that the length of the stone would be twice the width and twice the height of the cube. Its purpose is to lie across stones in walls to bind them together.

The broad oval may have been the Broached Thurnel, which will be discussed below, or as is stated in the *Chetwood Crawley* MS, a broaching maul or mallet or maul used to indent or furrow stone. In Samuel Pritchard's 1730 exposure of Freemasonry, *Masonry Dissected*, it is apparent that the third oval (i.e. third jewel) was not a tool but a second stone.[112] In *Masonry Dissected*, the following dialogue occurs:

> Q. What are the Immovable Jewels?
> A. Trasel Board, Rough Ashler, and Broach'd Thurnel.
> Q. What are their Uses?
> A. Trasel Board for the Master to draw his Designs upon, Rough Ashler for the Fellow Craft to try their Jewels upon, and the Broach'd Thurnel for the Enter'd 'Prentice to learn to work upon.[113]

The Broached Thurnel was a rough ashlar that had been worked upon (broached) to become a pointed cubical stone. The word "Thurnel" itself has an uncertain derivation. The perfect ashlar has now taken the place of the Broached Thurnel.[114] From 1744 in France and from the 1760s in England, the Smooth and Rough Ashlars were the two stones shown in the designs of lodge rooms.

This featuring of stone prominently displayed in the Lodge as the two ashlars, reaffirmed its symbolic centrality in Freemasonry.

Rock has a very specific Masonic significance as it also symbolizes soundness, good foundations, and wisdom, and the use of rocks is common in the highly symbolic Masonic gardens. The Masonic garden would create the symbolism and meaning of the Masonic Lodge in an outdoor setting. An inscription on the rock-work entrance to the Labyrinth at Worlitz, read *"Waehle Wandrer Deinen Weg Mit Verkunft"* or "Choose Traveler your path with Reason". This was symbolic of the path to be taken by the Masonic Initiate. The gardens of Worlitz contained a stone structure, the *Judentempel* or Jewish Temple. This was a circular building and symbolized a popular conception in the 17th and 18th centuries of the great stone Temple of Solomon in Jerusalem, the Masonic symbol of earthly perfection, as having been circular.[115]

Stone grottoes and caves were incorporated into Masonic gardens and by going through these, similar to going through a labyrinth, the Mason could recreate his Masonic journeys. These were constructed of rock which added to the symbolism and meaning of the experience. Although most of the gardens are now in ruins, the Masonic garden can still be experienced in the gardens of the *Quinta da Regaleira* in Sintra, Portugal. One descends a stone stairway seemingly deep into the earth. Entering a cave, it is necessary to walk carefully in the darkness, treading on stones set in a quiet stream of water. Upon turning a corner in the cave, one emerges into the light. It is an impressive recreation of the Entered Apprentice Degree of Freemasonry.

The impact of stone is also pronounced in various other Masonic Degrees, including the Mark Master, Most Excellent Master, and Royal Arch Degrees, which in the United States, together with the Past Master Degree, form the Chapter Degrees in the York Rite. In these degrees, the symbolic importance of stone is further experienced by the initiate in several different ways, each of which has an underlying powerful and deep theological basis.

The religious import of stone comes alive in the Mark Master Degree, where the keystone of the arch is rejected. The Mason is now working directly with stone, laboring symbolically in the mystical quarries of King Solomon's Temple. He becomes intimately involved in the symbolic resurrection of the rejected keystone in a deeply moving and spiritual ritual. It is the allegory of a reaffirmation of the search for that which was lost and by finding it, a commitment to Deity, the Great Architect of the Universe. The stone which the builders literally rejected is rescued by the Initiate and brought to the mystical Temple of Solomon to ultimately find its spiritual goal in becoming the keystone of the

Temple in its completion and dedication in the Most Excellent Master Degree which follows.

It is the stone quarry where the Initiate is sent as a place of spiritual refuge where he can add a spiritual component to his personal development. This will enable him to continue on in his Masonic journey.[116]

It is not only in the Mark Master Degree in which this deep spirituality exists but also in all of Freemasonry whose prime allegory is the working with stone to build the spiritual Temple of God. This is intensely personalized for each Mason, for each man must build his own spiritual Temple of stone. The Mason therefore works with spiritual stone to communicate directly with the Great Architect of the Universe as he builds this spiritual edifice. Each worthwhile act in his life puts the Mason in direct contact with Deity via the symbolic linkage of the spiritual building blocks of stone to each act of goodness and merit. As he places the symbolic stones in the spiritual edifice, the Mason is at one with Deity. He is truly at his *axis mundi*. Each Mason follows this personal spiritual path in his travels and advances through Freemasonry.

The Mark Master Degree also teaches through allegory it is the Great Architect of the Universe, and not man, who decides the spiritual wages that one shall receive for building this spiritual temple of stone when one at last arrives at the Celestial Lodge. Therefore, the spiritual stones that the Mason sets in place are also his communication to Deity who will have the final decision on the quality of the mystical edifice that the Mason has built painstakingly, spiritual stone by spiritual stone. When it is time for the mystical keystone to be inserted into the Great Arch of the Temple, it represents the work of the Mason throughout his lifetime, cutting, preparing, polishing, shaping and reshaping the keystone until it becomes the perfect stone, ready for the ultimate place in the perfection of his Celestial Temple.

In the Most Excellent Master Degree, the Temple is symbolically completed with the insertion of the Keystone into the Arch. It is a presentiment of what awaits the Mason in the Celestial Lodge as he completes his mystical spiritual Temple, that building not made with hands, eternal in the heavens.

In the Royal Arch Degree, which complements and completes the Master Mason Degree, three Initiates become three weary Hebrew sojourners from Babylonian exile and captivity, who travel the long and dusty road from Babylon to Jerusalem to assist in the rebuilding of the Temple. By undertaking the most menial tasks of clearing the rubble of the destroyed stones of the Temple of Solomon so that the Second Temple, the Temple of Zerubbabel, can be built, they make a startling discovery. Digging in the stone rubble, they find an impenetrable rock which has a hollow sound when struck. When the stone is lifted, a treasure of universal faith is discovered.

Lifting the stone is an ancient allegory of faith. In *The Sayings of Jesus*, a non-canonical Gospel found at site of the ancient Egyptian city, Oxyrhyncus, it was written:

> Lift up the stone and there shalt thou find me; cleave the wood and I am there.

Another example of something holy hidden beneath a stone is found in an old Irish folk-song *An Seann-Bhean*:

> Or is it true that the promises were written which Moses gave to the Jews
> And which King David placed timidly under the stone?[117]

This ritual of lifting of the stone was incorporated into Royal Arch Masonry at an early date. When John Coustos, an English Mason living in Lisbon was denounced to the Inquisition in Lisbon in 1742, his confessions to the Inquisitor, Manoel Varejao e Tavora, were recorded and the original documents were deposited in the Archives of the Inquisition. These were subsequently discovered and translated by a member of the Lisbon Branch of the Historical Association. Coustos' description of the Masonic ritual was quite accurate and in one part of his confession on March 26, 1743, he noted that:

> When the destruction took place of the famous Temple of Solomon there was found below the First Stone a tablet of bronze upon which was engraved JEHOVAH ...[118]

In this beautiful allegory in the Royal Arch Degree of the lifting of the stone, the three Masonic sojourners who symbolically lift the stone are led to the recovery of the Lost Masonic Word, the culmination of the Mason's search for the ultimate hierophany.

The symbolism of stone is therefore rich and varied with a religious and spiritual import that has the power to transform one's spiritual life. Throughout the history of man, it has been used as a hierophany, including the dwelling place of Deity, the spiritual approach to Deity, the source of creation of life, the source of magical power to invoke the powers of Deity, and as an often aniconic image of

Deity. It was not by accident that Freemasonry chose stone as the spiritual medium of Freemasonry.

In the 18th century world, in which there was still great intolerance, the Mark degree was a beacon for religious brotherhood. Through its unique ritual, it showed that men are capable of building this spiritual house of symbolic stone irrespective of their individual faith or creed. In the 16th and 17th centuries when Freemasonry developed, this concept, although in accord with the rationalistic spirit of the Age of Reason, was not the prevailing sentiment nor is it even today. If Freemasonry's message of spirituality and tolerance could be universally appreciated and followed, then truly, the message of the spirituality of stone could be fully understood.

CONCLUSIONS

Stone has been a powerful symbol since earliest times reflecting the ability of an inanimate object to possess a hierophany, the power of expressing something sacred. Various examples showing the hierophany of stone have been presented not only reflecting religious thought, but also from virtually every aspect of human creative endeavor dating back some 32,000 years to the dim mist of pre-history. Only by understanding this worldwide centrality of stone in religion and society can we appreciate the meaning of stone within Freemasonry and the ensuing powerful religious and spiritual messages found within Freemasonry derived from it. Freemasonry continues to use the allegorical meaning of stone in its rituals and philosophical precepts as working with stone is analogous to fulfilling the spiritual destinies of man. The Masonic work with stone is the counterpart of working to achieve the ultimate religious epiphany, that of the fulfilment of our spiritual goals in this world to prepare us for the ultimate reality of the world to come.

NOTES

1. Shepherd-Jones, G. S.: From Craft to Arch. In Turnbull, E. R. and Denslow, R. V.: *A History of Royal Arch Masonry.* Vol. 1. p. 491, Anchor Communications. Highland Springs, Virginia. 1956.

2. http://www.mystae.com/restricted/streams/gnosis/stones.html

3. Zeldis, L.Z.: *Masonic Symbols and Signposts.* p. 10, Anchor Communications. Lancaster, Va. 2003.

4. Durr, A.: Chicken and Egg—the Emblem Book and Freemasonry: the visual and Material Culture of Associate Life. *Ars Quatuor Coronatorum.* 118. pp 20–35, 2005.

5. Doniger,W.: Introduction to Eliade, M.: *Shamanism: Archaic Techniques of Ecstasy*, p. xiii. Princeton University Press. Princeton, 1964. Translated by Willard Trask from the French edition, *Le Chamanisme et les Techniques Archaïques de L'Extase*, Librairie Payot, Paris, 1951

6. von Franz, M.-L. in Jung, C. G.: *Man and His Symbols,* p. 226. Dell edition. 1968.

7. Eliade, M.: *Patterns in Comparative Religion*, p. 216, Lincoln, Neb.: U. of Nebraska Press, 1996 Translated from the French edition, *Traite d'histoire des Religions*, by Rosemary Sheed. Paris. Editions Payot.

8. Josephus: *Jewish Antiquities.* 2: 3. in *The New Complete Works of Josephus.* Translated by William Whiston. Kregel Publications. Grand Rapids. 1999

9. Eliade. *Patterns.* op. cit. p. 216

10. Chevalier, J. and Gheerbrant, A.: *The Penguin Dictionary of Symbols.* tr. John Buchanan-Brown. p, 933, Penguin Putnam. New York. 1996.

11. Stevens, A.: *Ariadne's Clue: A Guide to the Symbols of Humankind.* p. 112, Princeton University Press. Princeton, 2001

12. Frazer, J.: *The Golden Bough. A Study in Magic and Religion.* 1922.Abridged Edition. pp. 838–839. Penguin Books. 1996.

13. Stevens, A.: op. cit. p. 114.

14. Eliade. *Patterns* op. cit. pp. 217–219.

15. Biederman, H.: *Knaurs Lexicon der Symbole.* 1989. Tr. Hulbert, J.: *Dictionary of Symbolism.* pp. 219–220. Facts on File. New York. 1992

16. Stevens, A.: op. cit. p. 104,

17. Cirlot, J.E.: *A Dictionary of Symbols.* Trans. Jack Sage. p. 274,314. Dover Publications. Mineola, NY. 2002

18. Churton,T.: *The Golden Builders: Alchemists, Rosicrucians and the first Free Masons.* p. 18.Signal Publishing, Litchfield, Staffordshire. 2002

19. Frazer, J.: op. cit. p. 40.

20. Ibid., 228.

21. Ibid., p. 31.

22. Ibid., p. 40–41.

23. Ibid., pp. 91–97

24. Thom, B.: *Coast Salish Transformation Stories: Kinship, Place and Aboriginal Rights and Title in Canada.* Paper Presented at the 1998 Annual Meeting of the Canadian Anthropology Society, Toronto.

25. Frazer, J.: op. cit. pp. 694–695.

26. Stevens, A.: op. cit. p. 115.

27. Frazer, J.: *The Golden* op. cit. p. 19.

28. Ibid., p. 648.

29. Frazer, J.: op. cit. pp. 39–40.

30. Biederman, H.: op. cit. pp. 326–327.

31. Chevalier, J. and Gheerbrant, A.: op. cit. p. 937.

32. Wang, J.: *The Story of Stone: Intertextuality, Ancient Chinese Stone Lore, and the Stone Symbolism in Dream of the Red Chamber, Water Margin, and the Journey to the West.* pp. 50–60. Duke University Press. Durham. 1992.

33. Chevalier, J. and Gheerbrant, A.: op. cit. pp. 933–934.

34. http://www.gutenberg.com/eBooks/TonyKline_Collection/Html/Meta-morph.htm#_Toc64105467. Accessed December 2006.

35. Leeming, D.A.: *The World of Myth.* pp. 315–339. Oxford University Press. New York. 1990

36. Biederman, H.: op. cit. pp. 327–328.

37. Eliade. *Patterns.* op. cit. pp. 222–224.

38. Chevalier, J. and Gheerbrant, A.: op. cit. p. 935–936.

39. Frazer, J.: op. cit. p. 17.

40. Chevalier, J. and Gheerbrant, A.: op. cit. p. 937.

41. Stevens, A.: op. cit. p. 104

42. *The Jewish Encyclopedia.* pp. 558–559. Funk and Wagnalls, New York. 1904

43. Speth, G. W.: Builder's Rites and Ceremonies: The Folk-Lore of Masonry. Reprint of 1894 article. *Ars Quatuor Coronatorum.* 89. pp. 139–168, 1976.

44. Harvey, J.: *The Medieval Architect.* pp.226f. Cited In: Cryer, N. B.: *York Mysteries Revealed.* pp. 100–101. Ian Allen Printing. Surrey. 2006.

45. *The Holy Bible Containing the Old and New Testaments Commonly Known As the Authorized (King James) Version.* Genesis 28:22

46. Chevalier, J. and Gheerbrant, A.: op. cit. p. 933.

47. Ibid., p. 84,

48. Ibid., pp. 718–719

49. Eliade, M.: *Images and Symbols; Studies in Religious Symbolism.* p. 41, Princeton U. Press. Princeton,1991. Translated from the French edition, *Images et Symboles,* by Philip Mairet. Librairie Gallimard. Paris. 1952

50. Chevalier, J. and Gheerbrant, A.: op. cit. p. 83.

51. Ibid., p. 933.

52. Westcott, W. W.: *The Shamir.* Copy of unpublished manuscript. United Grand Lodge of England Library catalog number A180WES. 1910. Original manuscript 1888.

53. http://www.newadvent.org/cathen/08775b.htm

54. http://landru.i-link/shnyves/christian_symbolism.html

55. Smith, A.: in Moore, A. and Larkin, N., *Art at the Rockface. The Fascination of Stone.* Forward. Philip Wilson Publisher. London. 2006

56. Heyden, D.: Black Magic: Obsidian in Symbolism and Metaphor. In: Josserand, J. K. & Dakin, K.(eds). Smoke and Mist: Mesoamerican Studies in Memory of Thelma D. Sullivan. Vol.1. Oxford, B. A. R. International Series 402, 217–236. In: Williams, E.: Huichol Ethnography and Archeological Interpretation. *Papers for the Institute of Archeology.* 1. 6–15. 1990

57. Reed, C. A.: Ludic Revelations in the Enchanted Head Episode in Don Quixote (II, 62). *Bulletin of the Cervantes Society of America.* 24.1. 189–216. 2004

58. Thomas Aquinas, Saint: *The Summa theological of Saint Thomas Aquinas.* Trans. Fathers of the English Dominican Province. Vol. 13. 297–298. Burns, Oates, and Washbourne. London. 1932. in Reed: op. cit. p.206.

59. Clauss, J.: Review of Kerkhecker,A.: Callimachus' Book of Iambi. Oxford University Press. 1999, in *Bryn Mawr Classical Review.* 2001.07.12 in http://ccat.sas.upenn.edu/bmcr/2001–07–12.html. p.5

60. Cambrensis, G.: *The Itinerary of Archbishop Baldwin Through Wales.* Book II. {126}. In http://wwwworldwideschool.org/library/books/lit/historical/ItineraryofArchbishop_BaldwinThroughwales/chap17.html

61. http://en.wikipedia.org/wiki/Pasquinade.

62. http://www.artsmia.org/art-of-asia/architecture/chinese-scholars-study-in-room.cfm

63. http://www.worldwideschool.org/library/books/lit/poetry/ThePoems ofGoethe/chap22.html. Accessed Dec. 2006

64. Saslow, J.: *The Poetry of Michelangelo; An Annotated Translation.* Poem 152. p. 305. Yale University Press. New Haven. 1991.

65. Ibid., Poem 151, p. 302.

66. Scigliano, E.: *Michelangelo's Mountain: The Quest for Perfection in the Marble Quarries of Carrara.* p.24–29. Free Press. New York. 2005.

67. Saslow, J.: op cit. Poem 54. p. 142.

68. Hall, J.: *Michelangelo and the Reinvention of the Human Body.* pp. 28–33. Farrar, Straus, and Giroux. New York. 2005

69. http://www.italianstudies.org/poetry/st3.htm. Accessed December 2006

70. http://cessate.com Accessed December 2006.

71. Saslow, J.: op cit. Poem 124. p. 266.

72. http://www.dickens-literature.com/Our_Mutual_Friend/51.html. Accessed Nov. 2006

73. Clottes, J.: *Musée Des Roches.* Tr. Bennett, G.: *World Rock Art.* pp. 20–25. Getty Conservation Institute. Los Angeles. 2002.

74. Curtis, G.: *The Cave Painters: Probing the Mysteries of the World's First Artists.* p. 110. Alfred A. Knopf. New York. 2006.

75. Ibid., pp. 15–19.

76. Ibid., p. 77.

77. Ibid., p. 6.

78. Clottes, J.: *Musée Des Roches.* Tr. Bennett, G: *World Rock Art.* pp 69, 94–95. Getty Conservation Institute. Los Angeles. 2002.

79. Ellis, F. H. and Hammack. L.: The Inner Sanctum of Feather Cave, A Mogollon Sun and Earth Shrine linking Mexico and the Southwest. American Antiquity. 33(1): 25–44. Cited in Patterson, A.: *A Field Guide to Rock Symbols of the Greater Southwest.* p. 107. Johnson Books. Boulder. 1992.

80. Clottes, J.: Musée. Op cit., pp. 92–93.

81. http://www.classic-literature.co.uk/british-authors/16th-century/christopher-marlowe/dido-queen-of-carthage/ebook-page-04.asp

82. http://www.greece.org/cyprus/Iphis.htm.

83. Spenser, *The Faery Queen.* 1.7.36 http://www.stoics.com/spenser_s_faerie_queene_books_.html

84. Ibid., 2.2.9

85. Marlowe,C.: cited in http://etext.library.adelaide.edu.au/m/marlowe/christopher/tambur2/act4.html

86. Herrin, Lamar.: *Romancing Spain: A Memoir.* p. 87, Unbridled Books. Denver. 2006

87. Simic, C.: Stone. Cited in: http://project1.caryacademy.org/echoes/poet_Charles_Simic/samplepoemssimic.htm

88. http://www.worldwideschool.org/library/books/lit/poetry/LaysofAncientRome/chap4.html. Accessed December 2006,

89. http://poetry.poetryx.com/poems/784/

90. Lackner, M. A.: James Joyce, Freemasonry and Finnegan's Wake. *Transactions of the American Lodge of Research Free and Accepted Masons.* 30. pp. 55–81. 2001

91. Joyce, J.: *Ulysses,* 593. Vintage International ed. New York. 1990.ed. Modern Library. New York. 1934

92. Joyce, J.: *Finnegans Wake.* 123.34–124.3. Faber & Faber, 1939. Penguin Books ed. New York.1999

93. Ibid., 258:31–32.

94. Macalister, R.A.S.: *The Secret Languages of Ireland.* Cited in McHugh, R.: *Annotations to Finnegans Wake.* pp. 258–259. The Johns Hopkins University Press. Baltimore. 1980. Revised Edition 1991.

95. Joyce, J.: *Finnegans Wake.* op. cit. 258:28–259:2.

96. http://multivalent.sourceforge.net/format/pdf/Aida.pdf. p.32. Accessed Nov. 2006.

97. Eldridge, R.: "Hidden Secrets of the Self": E. T. A. Hoffman's Reading of Don *Giovanni* In Goehr, L. and Herwitz, D.: *The Don Giovanni Moment.* pp. 33–46, Columbia U. Press. New York, 2006.

98. Henahan, D.: *Opera: The Stone Guest.* The New York Times Archive. Feb.27, 1986

99. Kenyon, N.: *The Faber Guide to Mozart*, p. 328. Faber and Faber. London. 2005

100. Grey, T.S.: The Gothic Libertine: The Shadow of Don Giovanni in Romantic Music and Culture. In Goehr, L. and Herwitz, D.: op. cit. pp. 76–79.

101. Gasparov, N.: *Don* Juan in Nicholas's Russia (Pushkin's the Stone Guest). In Goehr, L. and Herwitz, D.: op. cit. pp. 46–56.

102. Cairns, D.: *Mozart and His Operas.* p. 163. U. of California Press. Berkeley. 2006.

103. Kenyon, N.: op. cit. p. 331.

104. Hesse, H.: *Steppenwolf.* p. 204. Picador Henry Holt & Co. 1963. Originally published by Fischer-Verlag A.G. Berlin.

105. Bacht, N.: Adorno and the Don. In Goehr, L. and Herwitz, D.: op. cit. p. 230.

106.Béresniak, B.: *Symbols of Freemasonry.* pp. 22–24. Assouline Publishing. New York. 2000. Translated by Ian Monk from *Les Symboles des Francs-Maçons*, Editions Assouline. 1997

107.*Florida Masonic Monitor.* p. 94. 1994.

108.Ibid., pp. 39–40.

109.Cryder, N.B.: *The Arch and the Rainbow.* pp. 170–171. Ian Allan Regalia. Addlestone. 1996.

110.Ibid., p. 33.

111.Jones, B. E.: *Freemasons' Book of the Royal Arch* p. 410. George G. Harrup/ London. 1957. New and Revised Edition. Eric Dobby Publishing. 1956.

112.Carr, H.: *The Freemason At Work.* pp. 338–339. Lewis Masonic, London. 1976. Revised by Smyth, F. Seventh ed. 1996

113.Pritchard, S.: Masonry Dissected. p. 14. J. Wilford. 1730. In Carr, H.: *Harry Carr's World of Freemasonry.* Appendix. Lewis Masonic. Shepperton, Middlesex. 1984

114.Jones, B. E.: *Freemasons' Guide and Compendium* pp. 413–414. Harrup Ltd. London. 1950. New and Revised Edition. Eric Dobby Publishing. 1956

115.Curl, J.S.: *The Art & Architecture of Freemasonry.* pp. 180–181. Overlook Press. NY 2002.

116.Graham, E. R.: *The History and Symbolism of Royal Arch Masonry.* p.45. 1st Books. 2000.

117.Jones, B. E.: *Freemasons' Book of the Royal Arch.* op. cit. pp. 44–45.

118.Dashwood, J. R.: The Trial of John Coustos. *Ars Quatuor Coronatorum.* 66. pp. 107–123, 1953.

'THE SPIRIT OF ASSOCIATION': FREEMASONRY AND EARLY TRADE UNIONS

◆

BY ANDREW PRESCOTT, Ph.D

In studying the social history of England in the early nineteenth century, it sometimes seems that every path leads to the name of Francis Place. Whether one is
interested in education, economics, birth control or popular customs, the name
of Place quickly crops up. Place was a tailor of Charing Cross who became a leading radical politician and a friend of Jeremy Bentham and John Stuart Mill. He
was an assiduous archivist, and left a huge collection of papers bearing on almost
every aspect of early nineteenth century social history, which is now in the British
Library. Place's greatest achievement was undoubtedly his role in the repeal of the
mass of legislation, known as the Combination Acts, which restricted the rights
of both employers and workers to form associations for the purposes of control-
ling and regulating working conditions. Place was largely responsible for organis-
ing the presentation of evidence to a select committee in 1824 which led to the
successful passage of a bill repealing this legislation. He was equally energetic
again in the following year in ensuring that a further select committee did not
completely overturn this victory.

In 1834, Place recalled the effects of the combination laws, in the following
words: 'Everything on the part of the workmen was done by stealth before the
repeal of the Combination Laws, and in contravention to the laws, which were
unjust and exceedingly severe; workmen could not meet openly to adjust any
matter relating to their business. If a few met and wished to come to an understanding with the masters, they were prosecuted, not always under the Combina-

tion Laws, but at common law, and very severe sentences were passed upon them. The men had to a very great extent oaths of secrecy, all their discussions were secret, and this course of conduct demoralised them very much; it was a great impediment to their improvement, and did no good to the masters'.

Oaths tended to make parliamentary committees nervous, and it reflects Place's adroit handling of the witnesses before the 1824 and 1825 enquiries that the issue of the use of oaths and initiation rituals by workmen's groups does not loom very large in the evidence taken by these committees. The most substantial discussion occurred as a result of evidence given by Alexander Guthrie, the manager of the Duke of Portland's collieries in Ayrshire. Guthrie said that an association of colliers had been formed, which required its members to swear an oath and used passwords and secret signs. He repeated the oath which was as follows: 'I do solemnly swear, before God and those who trow, that I will haill, conceal, and never reveal this secret of word, sign and grip; that I will not write it, cut or carve, print it or engrave it, mark or stain it, upon anything that will bear a mark, or the meaning of a letter; and I will always assist a brother collier in anything I can help him in, if consistent with my own safety; and I will assist the Glasgow Clydesdale Operative Brethren, if consistent with reason, equity and justice, and consistent with the laws of my country; and that I will not make, or see any made, under the number Three, and not then until represented with a good moral character. Now, as I have sworn, may the Lord enable me to perform this my obligation'.

Guthrie said that the password then in use was 'Mizpah', and described the grips used by the colliers: 'The signs are to touch the right ear with the right thumb and forefinger, and answered by the other person putting down his right hand by his left side, in allusion to Malchus's ear being cut off, and Jesus enjoining Peter to put up his sword. The grips formerly used were few in number, called Clerk the Boards or shovel, the pick, the wedge and the mell; but of late a new one has been formed, called the reversed sign, which is done by the one person putting up the right hand middle finger, while the other holds his hand out and right middle finger down.'

This was the kind of evidence which was potentially dangerous to those advocating repeal of the Combination Laws, and one can sense Francis Place working frantically behind the scenes to secure the appearance before the committee of William McAllister, a worker from the Kilmarnock Coal Works, who was able to put the information provided by Guthrie in a completely different light. McAllister denied that the miners' association had any secret bye laws and regulations, and said that oaths were not used. He was asked if any secret signs were used for recognition. He replied 'Yes but that does not belong to this association'. McAllister was asked what organisation used the signs. He said that they were to do with 'the Brotherhood of the Colliery, that has nothing to do with this association'. I will quote the evidence verbatim:

'What is the Nature of the Brotherhood of the Colliery? It is the same as freemasonry.

How far does it extend? It extends just among the colliers themselves.

What is the intention of it? Just to make them friendly and true to each other.

Has it anything to do with striking? Nothing in the world.

Has it nothing to do with supporting one another in the case of a strike? No.

Of what number may the Brotherhood consist? It may consist of every collier in the world.

McAllister was shown the oath which had been produced by Guthrie, and declared that it was not the oath used by the Brotherhood. Unfortunately, McAllister felt that he could not repeat the true oath. He was asked again:

'Do you conceive it the same as free masonry? It is the same.

Are you a free mason? Yes', replied McAllister.

Thus McAllister sought to rebut Guthrie's charges by suggesting that the oaths and secret signs were connected, not with the trade union, but rather with a separate organisation whose purpose was purely social. Doubts may be felt about whether McAllister was being disingenuous in making this distinction. Firm lines of this sort were not always drawn in the early nineteenth century workplace. Place himself describes how he entered radical politics by becoming secretary of the Breeches Makers Benefit Society, a club which was ostensibly meant to support members when sick and bury them when dead, but which was really, in Place's words, 'intended for the purpose of supporting the members in a strike for wages'. Likewise, the Scottish colliers probably did not make as strong a distinction between their union and the brotherhood as McAllister suggested. This Brotherhood was apparently also found in England. Another witness refers to the prevalence among miners in North Shields of the system known as brothering: 'They bound themselves to obey the orders of the brotherhood at the peril of their lives, on the penalty of being stabbed through the heart, or their bowels ripped up'.

Place and his fellow radicals hoped that, once the Combination Laws were repealed, workers associations would no longer feel the need for secret oaths and passwords, and would become respectable and progressive organisations, enabling workers to become a well-organised and sober part of a system of laisser-faire economics. However, the growth in popularity of trades unions in the 1820s and

1830s was accompanied by an upsurge in the use of oaths and ritual. Indeed, it may be that, far from prompting unions to abandon ceremonial and secrecy, the repeal of the Combination Laws made members of unions feel that they could safely adopt such proceedings. Raymond Postgate points out that the Society of Preston Joiners had carried on without any ritual from 1807 to 1833. In 1833, the Society purchased a 'Square and Compasses', and provided a subsidiary lodge at Kendal with regalia for the purposes of initiation. When the Society became part of the Operative Builders Union, there was further substantial expenditure on regalia as well as on the purchase of a new top coat, a cocked hat and false moustaches for the tyler. In forming the Grand National Consolidated Trades Union, the social visionary Robert Owen protested against the use of initiation ceremonies as 'relics of barbarism', but was persuaded that they were necessary as a 'temporary concession to ignorance'.

Another opponent of such ceremonial was the republican and atheist Richard Carlile, the chief populariser of the works of Thomas Paine. Carlile is, of course, known to masonic scholars for his *Manual of Freemasonry*, an exposure of freemasonry first published in Carlile's journal *The Republican* while he was a prisoner in Dorchester gaol in 1825. In *The Republican*, Carlile had adopted a standard materialist criticism of masonic ritual as useless mummery, and had criticised masonic oaths as a potentially corrupting influence. His stance had subsequently shifted, however, and under the influence of both Paine and the pioneer of comparative religion Godfrey Higgins, Carlile had come to view masonic ritual as embodying remnants of the ancient pre-christian sun religion. He was unable, however, to trace any such exalted origins for trade union ritual.

In December 1833, Carlile published in his journal *The Gauntlet* (subtitled 'A Sound Republican London Weekly Paper') a leading article on trades unions. Carlile could hardly disapprove of the unions, but he felt they were just a beginning, 'mere embryonic mental and physical struggles for a better state of human existence'. 'Though weak, crude, sickly and comparatively helpless in their birth', wrote Carlile, 'they will, under good care and proper education, grow up into a manhood capable of independence and determined to have a common justice in the social sphere'. However, there was something that Carlile felt required immediate attention: 'There is one thing very desirable to be done at once for and by these trades' unions', he wrote, 'and that is to break up their secret character, their oaths and ceremonial nonsense. Some little excitement was created on Monday, in consequence of the arrest, in the streets, of some persons, who late at night had in bags the paraphenalia of a lodge, as the meetings of the unions are now called, in imitation of the Masonic, Orange, and Odd Fellows' mischief and nonsense. Two persons having the bags of the lodge were stopped by a policeman, demanding to know what they had got. The members of the union answered that it was no business of the policeman's. He took them to the station house. They gave the same answer to the inspector. He examined their bags, and the first thing presenting itself was a battle axe'. Carlile urged the unions to abandon these procedures; while they retained such ritual, he declared, 'they may be feared, but they will never be respected'. Carlile was to have occasion to return to this subject again over the next few months.

At the end of January 1834, Carlile visited Plymouth on a lecture tour. Carlile's own appearance—as a notorious infidel and radical—caused excitement enough, but while he was there events in Exeter caused an even greater stir. *The Gauntlet* carried the relevant report from the *Plymouth Herald*. The Exeter police had heard rumours that representatives of the Operative Builders' Union were actively recruiting in the area. They established that a meeting would be taking place on 15th January in the Sun Inn. The captain of the watch hid himself in a next door room, and made a hole in the wall so he could see what was going on. After about fifty men had gathered in the room, it was announced that a ceremony of initiation would take place. The captain immediately left his hiding place and rushed off to fetch reinforcements. After a great struggle, the police managed to force their way into the room where the meeting was in progress. The lights were extinguished and a number of men escaped by jumping from the windows. Eventually, about forty men were arrested.

The *Herald* went on to describe what was found in the room: 'On the table in the room lay the Bible open, and a Testament, a manuscript book of proceedings, the oath of initiation, letters, papers, et cetera. There were also formed of wood, sundry representations of ancient battle axes, one of them with a double head, having a handle several feet in length, and two swords of the description formerly used by our light dragoons. Besides these were two masks appended to wigs or covers for the head, formed of sheep skin, with the wool outwards, somewhat after the manner of a judge's wig; and two flowing white garments after the manner of surplices. But the masterpiece in the way of the terrific, was a gaunt figure of Death, painted on canvas, of from six to seven feet in height; the right arm of the figure being raised above the head, and the hand furnished with a dart, with which it appears about to transfix the person standing before it; an inscription above having the words 'Remember Thy Latter End'. At the foot on one side, is an hour glass, and on the other the terrestial globe'. At the time the police burst in, three men had been blindfolded.

The ceremony used was presumably similar to that in a manuscript dating from 1831 used by the Society of Operative Stone Masons, a component part of the Operative Builders Union. There isn't time here to give a full description of the ritual, but, as Andy Durr has commented, although the oath was in a fairly simple form, 'there is no doubt that the ritual surrounding the obligation was meant to impress. The initiate was brought in blindfolded and went through a long ceremony, and when the blindfold was removed he was faced with the officers of the Lodge in regalia, one holding a gilded axe'. Carlile, as a result of his study of masonic ritual, had no doubt where the ceremony was derived from: 'It is a paltry imitation of masonic proceedings', he declared. He felt that the union members were 'making great fools of themselves'. Eventually fifteen of those arrested at Exeter were sent for trial on a charge of 'combining and confederating themselves together for the purpose of effecting an unlawful object'. They admitted their guilt at the assizes, and were bound over. This comparatively lenient treatment may have been due to events a few weeks later not far away in Dorset, which made the question of union oaths even more contentious.

In March 1834, six Dorsetshire farm labourers were tried at the Dorchester assizes for 'administering and causing to be administered, and aiding and assisting, at being present at, and consenting to administer, a certain unlawful oath and engagement'. The labourers had formed an 'Agricultural Friendly Society' which involved an initiation rite, described by one of the witnesses against them: 'One of the prisoners asked if we were ready to have our eyes blindfolded; we said 'Yes'; we then (all five of us) bound our handkerchiefs round our eyes; we were then led by a person through a passage into another room, on the same floor; on getting into that room a paper was read to us, but I do not recollect any of the words that were read; after the paper had been read we knelt down on being desired to do so; something else was then read to us; the voice which read appeared to be the same; I don't know what the reading was about; but I think it was from some part of the Bible; we then got up, turned ourselves around and took the bandage from our eyes being desired to do so; a light was in the room; I saw in a corner of the room something (a picture, I think) which had the appearance of a skeleton; on looking at that picture James Loveless said, 'Remember Your End'. We were then desired to blind our eyes again and to kneel down; the same voice read again something which I don't remember; we were afterwards desired to kiss a book; our eyes were then unblinded; I then saw all the prisoners present; some of them were sitting, some standing; James Loveless had then a different dress from what he now has on ... 'The witness was asked in cross-examination whether he had ever been an oddfellow or a freemason, which he denied.

The prisoners were, of course, the Tolpuddle Martyrs, whose actions in carrying out this initiation and administering this oath was to earn them a sentence of seven years transportation to Australia. The sentence unleashed a storm of protest, which in the end resulted in the labourers receiving pardons after they had been in Australia for nearly two years. As Richard Carlile observed, the case 'all turned upon the oath making'. Some radical journals tried to make light of this, one even denying that an oath had been administered, but for Carlile it confirmed his suspicions of the trade unions—'a greater piece of quackery has never been played off upon mankind', he declared, and the last issue of the *Gauntlet* had on the front page a grotesque engraving of the initiation, with a blunt declaration by Carlile: 'You have degraded yourselves. I present you today with a picture of your degradation. Some men learn better by pictures than by letters'. If you want nonsense, said Carlile, why pay more when you could buy his exposure of freemasonry for five shillings?

In setting up research centres into freemasonry, such as the centre here at Canonbury or the new Centre at Sheffield, I and others have naturally emphasised the lack of attention paid to the history of freemasonry by professional scholars in England. However, one can easily exaggerate the situation and give the impression that professional historians have ignored freemasonry altogether, which is not the case. Particularly striking is the way in which interesting and suggestive references to freemasonry are made by historians of the left, such as Eric Hobsbawm, E. P. Thompson, Gwyn Williams, Raymond Postgate, and Raphael Samuel. These allusions to freemasonry point towards themes and connections which certainly deserve closer investigation.

In looking for interesting starting points on the history of freemasonry, one would not expect to turn to such classic works of left wing historiography as Sidney and Beatrice Webb's *History of Trade Unionism* or Raymond Postgate's *The Builders' History*, but the issue of the use of ritual by trade unions means that freemasonry is discussed early in these volumes, and its treatment is interesting. The Webbs had a profound effect on the study of early trade union history by their insistence that there was no connection between trade unions and the medieval guilds. The Webbs' outlook is summarised by the following quote: 'We assert with some confidence that in no case did any trade union in the United Kingdom arise either directly or indirectly by descent from a craft gild'. This conclusion partly reflected the way in which the Webbs defined trade unions. According to the Webbs, true trade unions were 'continuous associations' and the early bodies were, in their opinion, more ephemeral, so that they were, by definition, not trade unions. The Webbs stated that trade unions first appeared in the late seven-

teenth century, and until recently, few disagreed with this view. The parallels
with the way in which, by similar manipulation of definitions, the history of freemasonry has also been taken by many English masonic scholars to begin in the
late seventeenth century are very striking.

The reason for the Webbs insistence on the late emergence of trades unions
was that their work was first published when the new unions, with their mass
semi-skilled and unskilled membership, were beginning to displace the older
craft-based unions. The Webbs were anxious to support the new unions, with
their emphasis on greater political action, and did not wish to emphasise the
older roots of union activity. The oaths and rituals of trade unions in the 1820s
and 1830s were worryingly suggestive of a medieval tradition, and it suited the
Webbs' purpose to suggest that they might have been an import from an exotic
institution from freemasonry. As Robert Leeson has put it, 'The Webbs, unwill-
ing to accept the direct transmission of craft traditions, argued that early union
'ritual and regalia' was borrowed from the 'small friendly societies' around them
… they tried to prove that the Operative Builders Union in 1834 took its clearly
building trade ritual from the Leeds Woolcombers, who got it from the Rochdale
Flannel Weavers, who got it from the Oddfellows' Friendly Society, who borrowed it from the Freemasons'.

While historians of trade unions have, for their own reasons, been quick to
suggest links between early trade union ritual and freemasonry, masonic scholars
have been less interested. With the exception of an article by B. Springett in *The
Freemason* in 1925, the subject was largely neglected by masonic scholars until
1987, when Andy Durr finally gave the subject its proper due in a wonderful article in *Ars Quatuor Coronatorum*, entitled 'Ritual of Association and Organisations of the Common People'. This article gives a comprehensive overview of the
use of rituals among union movements. Durr emphasises how ritual has proved a
much more tenacious feature of union life than many labour historians have been
willing to admit. He points out that the boilermakers and blacksmiths were still
using ritual initiation at the beginning of the twentieth century, and notes that in
1963, when the boilermakers, blacksmiths and shipwrights formed a new union,
they issued a new ritual book, which was still in use in 1987. Durr also emphasises the link between the use of ritual in unions and the practices of friendly societies such as the Oddfellows, Ancient Order of Druids and the Free Gardeners.
Durr's article is a major contribution to the history of trade unions. It is sometimes lamented that articles in AQC are not used by historians, but Durr's article
shows how, if an article in AQC addresses problems in which historians are interested, it will be used and cited by them—Durr's article duly receives pride of

place in the bibliography of Malcolm Chase's recent monograph on *Early Trade Unionism*.

Despite the importance of Durr's article, it is striking that masons only seem to have remembered the possible links with the unions at a time when freemasonry was in trouble—Durr's article is framed explicitly in terms of developing a response to the publication of Stephen Knight's book *The Brotherhood*. Moreover, although historians of freemasonry, friendly societies and trade unions have all noticed the parallels between their different rituals, little attention has been paid to the interaction between this different organisations and the effect it had on them. How did freemasons feel when they heard about the Tolpuddle Martyrs using forms of oath which reflected, however distantly, masonic forms? And what effect did this reaction have on both organisations?

Although freemasons today may be happy to note the links with trade unions and friendly societies, this was by no means the case in the nineteenth century. A letter from the archives at Great Queen Street illustrates the kind of tensions which might arise. The institution of the tramp dates back perhaps to the middle ages. Artisans who were out of work would undertake on foot a tour of towns. Their fellow craftsmen would give them work if there was any available. If not, the tramp would receive food, money and a bed for the night. One of the major functions of trade unions was the organisation of this system, which in the first half of the nineteenth century achieved its most elaborate form, with a system of designated houses of call and elaborate printed passport-like documents issued to travelling members to record their journeys. (Many of the Masons' Arms pub names which still survive derive, not from connections with freemasons, but because they were houses of call for operative stonemasons on the tramp). Benefits to tramps were not only dispensed by craft organisations. Friendly societies like the Oddfellows also offered relief to travelling members.

In 1816, Charles Whiteley, a freemason who held provincial office in Lancashire, wrote to the Grand Secretary in London to express his concern about help given to tramps who were freemasons. He wrote that 'Of late we have had many applications from tramps for relief, and some only recently initiated who considered they had a right to relief as they pretended they were seeking work'. Whiteley was worried that some of these men were active unionists, and expressed his anxiety that 'should it be known that these people are masons it will be considered that the craft are supporters of illegal combinations among workmen'. Whiteley illustrated the sort of abuse he was worried about by describing a conversation he had had with a tramp who recently called at his factory. 'I recollected having seen him some six months before on the same errand. He informed me that he had travelled since the time he was here before nearly all over this kingdom, also Ireland and part of Scotland, and had saved money by it. As he was an Orangeman and an Odd Fellow he had been relieved by them and he meant to be made a mason when he got home which was in the neighbourhood of Stockport'. Whiteley's letter expresses a concern to distinguish freemasonry from mere friendly societies and, above all, from trade unions, which was a common feeling among freemasons during the first half of the nineteenth century, and was to have important repercussions on all sides right up to the present day.

In understanding the relationship between freemasonry, friendly societies and trade unions in the nineteenth century, the key text is the Unlawful Societies Act of 1799, about which some of you may have heard me speak at the Canonbury conference last year. This act was one of the various measures introduced by Pitt's government to stifle the threat of revolution in the wake of events in France. The 1799 act was a direct response to the activities of such revolutionary bodies as the United Irishmen and the Corresponding Societies. The Unlawful Societies Act outlawed bodies which administered unlawful oaths (as defined in an earlier act of 1797). It also outlawed organisations which held closed meetings and were organised into branches with national committees. Membership of such bodies was punishable with seven years transportation. The only people excepted from this law were the freemasons. The exemption for the freemasons had been hurriedly agreed at committee stage, and an original proposal for regulation by the grand lodges had been overturned in the House of Lords, to be replaced with a system requiring registration of lodges with the clerk of the peace. The 1799 Act entered the statute book on 12 July, the same day as the notorious Combination Act, which facilitated summary procedure against trades unions. It seems that this was purely coincidental, but it nevertheless presaged the significant role the 1799 act was to play in the history of working class organisations.

The exemption for freemasons under the 1799 act created a gulf between freemasonry and other analogous organisations. The Grand Lodges in England and Scotland were able to use the 1799 act to tighten their control over the organisation of freemasonry, so that in Scotland the act was used to eradicate the Royal Arch and higher degrees, and an unsuccessful attempt was made to wipe out Lodge Mother Kilwinning. The 1799 act was thus within freemasonry a force for centralisation. By contrast, for organisations which fell outside the scope of the 1799 act, the act temporarily wiped out any national organisation and made it difficult to continue with the working of ritual. This was a problem even where organisations were specifically permitted by other legislation, such as friendly societies. The Oddfellows were the first to discover this. In June 1799, the

United Order of Odd Fellows submitted their 'general laws' for scrutiny to the Home Office. The Home Office sought systematically to open up meetings and remove much of the ritual. For example, the second clause ordered that 'the Noble Grand examine every stranger that shall go to the lodge room at the time the lodge is opened; and after the lodge is opened, the guardian shall demand the word, or sign, from any stranger who wishes to be admitted'. The Home Office officials simply struck this through as unacceptable. The rule stating that any brother who revealed the secrets of the order would be expelled was similarly struck down. The word 'making' was changed to 'admission' throughout, and references to the use of oaths removed.

The 1799 act was remembered in the traditions of oddfellowship as devastating the national organisation. R. Moffrey in his *Century of Oddfellowship* declared that 'So stringent was the administration of this act through the medium of spies and common informers that the frail ties which bound the branches to the Grand Lodges were severed, records destroyed, and all traces of the lodges as branches of their order were lost'. Moffrey saw the attack on ritual as particularly lamentable 'and hence we have lost, except as a literary fact, one of the most impressive modes of educating grown men'. Other friendly societies apparently suffered in a similar way. In 1823, a magistrate at Chelmsford expressed concern about the activities of the Druids in the area, and the Home Office advised that proceedings should be taken against them under the 1799 Act (which had been reissued in 1817). Progressive splits in the Druids from 1800 were probably due to anxiety about the illegality of the unregistered society

The 1799 legislation also created difficulties for the Orange order in England. This spread from Ireland by means of military lodges, and in England seems to have functioned at first very much as a protestant friendly society. When a query was raised about the existence of an Orange lodge among members of the West York militia, the commanding officer wrote that 'The Lodge has existed for ten years in this regiment; it is a society of loyal and philanthropic tendency like free masonry. There are, I understand, similar lodges held in many regiments and most towns of the kingdom'. Nevertheless, when the head of the London Orange Orders applied for a military commission and mentioned his membership of the order, it was pointed out to him by the Home Office that 'it being considered that oaths are administered to members of Orange Societies, it is thought right that he should be informed that all such oaths are illegal.' Under the terms of the 1799 act, members of Orange lodges were, declared the Home Secretary, 'liable to imprisonment and transportation.'

Although there were numerous prosecutions under the combination laws prior to 1824, the 1799 legislation, with its sanctions against oaths and the formation of societies with different branches, also provided a weapon against the unions, and was used where the government and local magistrates were apprehensive that union activities might be linked to radical protests. In 1802, a member of a shearmen's club in Yorkshire was prosecuted for swearing an oath 'to be true to the shearmen, and to see that none of them are hurt, and not to divulge any of their secrets'. In 1804, a prosecution was brought by the Master Boot and Shoe Makers in London against the association of journeymen boot and shoe makers under the terms of 1799 act, on the grounds that, as a body with elected officials, the society was illegal. Fundamentally, the Combination Laws seem to have been regarded as suitable for dealing with small local associations, but the 1799 legislation was preferred where there was any suggestion of a large organisation, with branches and elected committees. This is evident from an opinion given by the Treasury Solicitor in 1811 concerning a combination of framework knitters in the Midlands: 'the meetings alluded to … are not within the purview of the Act 39 George III, chapter 79, although they are not prepared to say that they may not be brought within the words of it. They think the attention of the magistrates should be called to 39 George III, chapter 81, expressly made for the suppression of combinations of workmen …

With the repeal of the Combination Laws, the 1799 act, as restated and refined in 1817, was nevertheless left on the statute book, and still offered a powerful weapon against the formation of larger unions. The 1799 act, in outlawing secret oaths, referred back to piece of legislation two years previously which made it a felony to administer an oath binding a person not to reveal an unlawful confederacy. It was the 1797 and 1799 statutes which were used against the Tolpuddle Martyrs. The Tolpuddle Martyrs themselves were, of course, unaware that their actions were illegal; as far as they were concerned, the Combination Laws had been repealed. Consequently, it is usually suggested that they were prosecuted as a result of a vindictive government, prompted by a vicious magistrate, remembering a half-forgotten piece of legislation, but this is far from being the case—in proceeding down this route against the Dorchester labourers, the law officers were following a path against trade unions which had been well worn since 1799.

The implications of the use of the 1799 legislation against the Tolpuddle Martyrs were not lost on other organisations affected by its terms. The only organisation with an exemption from the 1799 act were the freemasons, although this had been extended in 1817 to cover meetings of Quakers as well. The exemption for the freemasons was dependent on lodges regularly submitting returns of their membership to the clerk of the peace. As soon as news of events in Dorset broke, United Grand Lodge in England moved quickly to ensure that all lodges were duly registered. The Grand Master at that time, the Duke of Sussex, was suffering from cataracts, and had been excused attendance from court. Nevertheless, he went out of his way to attend a Grand Festival on 30th April 1834 to comment on the situation. The Freemasons Quarterly Review reported his speech as follows: 'In consequence of late events, I have deemed it advisable, by a circular to the master of every lodge, to call the attention of the craft to that Act of George III which protects the assemblies of masons, and directs that the number and place of meeting of every lodge should be left with the Clerk of the Peace. That complied with, masons are exempt from all interference by the statutes which have been enacted for the suppression of secret societies. In this proceeding, I have been actuated by a desire to preserve a due obedience to the laws by which the order has been protected and supported, and extend the respectability and high character of the craft.'

In proposing a toast to the Duke, Lord Durham made an interesting allusion to the use of ritual by the unions: 'Let those who had borrowed the language of their societies from the craft, imitate their love of order, their obedience to the laws, and ever peaceable conduct; and neither of the parties would regret, the mason, that his precepts had been copied, or the communities that had followed such pure examples'. The seriousness with which United Grand Lodge viewed the need to protect is legal exemption is apparent from the urgent language of the circular, which required lodges to register with the Clerk of the Peace immediately on receipt of the circular, and to inform United Grand Lodge immediately they had done so.

One of the chief supporters of the Tolpuddle Martyrs was Henry Hetherington, whose journal *The Poor Man's Guardian* played the leading role in the campaign for their pardon. Hetherington, like others, had been quick to point out that oaths and ritual were not limited to trade unionists: 'Combination is practiced by all classes', he wrote, 'and, as to oath administering, it is usual with the Freemasons, the Oddfellows, the Orangemen of Ireland, and various other societies'. On 24 May, the Poor Man's Guardian reported the receipt by a masonic lodge in Bury of the Duke of Sussex's circular instructing lodges to register with the Clerk of the Peace. Hetherington reported rumours that the circular was intended as a step towards 'the putting down of all spurious lodges, whether of trade unions or secret societies'. This gave Hetherington the occasion for a lively editorial accusing the freemasons of seeking to protect their own position by supporting despotic acts and declaring that the unions would never submit to any attempt to outlaw them. Hetherington suspected that the masonic circular presaged legislation from the government which would extend its powers to suppress societies. His fears were probably exaggerated, but it is possible that the Duke of Sussex, in issuing the circular, may have been anticipating a campaign of prosecutions under the 1799 act to suppress closed societies.

If the prosecution of the Tolpuddle Martyrs created alarms for the freemasons, it was even more disconcerting for the Oddfellows, who were mentioned in the press as an example of a body administering oaths as frequently as the masons, but who, unlike the masons, enjoyed no legal protection. From about 1810, the Oddfellows had began gradually to reestablish a national form of organisation with the rise of the Manchester Unity, although this was constantly subject to splits and schisms. The Oddfellows sought to demonstrate their respectability by extravagant protestations of loyalty, matching United Grand Lodge in their assiduousness in making loyal addresses to the throne. At the time of the trial of the Tolpuddle Martyrs, the Annual Moveable Committee of the Manchester Unity was meeting at Hull, and the trial seems to have produced something of a panic among the Oddfellows. According to the *Manual of Oddfellowship*, 'such was the terror produced by the result of the trial, that the Directors resolved to abandon the system previously existing, and destroy every vestige [of ceremony] that could be construed into anything likely to compromise the order. The effect of English legislation did not extend to the United States, and therefore the American Independent Order was able to retain the ritual … 'All the degrees which had been gradually reintroduced since 1799 were abolished, and replaced with much simpler lectures.

The trial of the Tolpuddle Martyrs caused similar alarm in the British Orange movement. The question of the legal status of the Orange organisation was discussed at a meeting of Grand Lodge in June 1834, but the Orangemen believed they were on reasonably safe ground, since they administered no oath as such, but instead required members to take an oath of allegiance and supremacy before a magistrate. Nevertheless, they took the precaution of ordering a new edition of the rules to be printed in which minor alterations were made better to secure their legality. Notwithstanding these actions, the Orange movement in England, of which the Duke of Cumberland was Grand Master, was about to run into increasing difficulties. Many were alarmed by the possibility that Victoria could accede to the throne while still a minor so that the country would be governed by a regent such as the Duke of Wellington. There were persistent rumours that the Duke of Cumberland intended to use the Orangemen to stage a coup to prevent this happening. The existence of many regimental lodges encouraged fears that the Orange order could carry out a military coup. In 1835, there was a parliamentary inquiry into Orangeism. Under pressure in the House of Commons to take action, the government asked royal permission to use the 1799 legislation against the Orange order. William IV indicated that he would support such action, whereupon, at the end of February 1836, the Duke of Cumberland dissolved all the Orange lodges in England.

It was the proceedings against the Orange Order which provided the means of reopening the case of the Tolpuddle Martyrs. At the time of the dissolution of the Orange lodges, Sir William Molesworth made a speech in parliament pointing out that the Dorsetshire labourers had been condemned for a far more innocent act. The difference was that their chief, unlike the Orangemen, had not been a prince of the blood. In a letter to the Prime Minister, Lord Melbourne, the Home Secretary, Lord John Russell, admitted that 'To be sure the Duke of Cumberland and the Duke of Gordon are far more guilty than the labourers, but the law does not reach them, I fear'. The labourers were pardoned shortly afterwards.

The Webbs assumed that the case of the Tolpuddle Martyrs marked the end of the use of ceremonies of initiation by unions. Andy Durr has illustrated how the use of such ritual proved much more long-lived, and has still not completely died out. The union rituals were, however, constantly subject to attack and attrition in the face of legislative pressures and the concern of Victorian union leaders to emphasise their respectability. Unions constantly either abolished or simplified the ritual. In 1838, in response to a further parliamentary inquiry into trades unions as a result of criminal activity attributed to the Glasgow cotton-spinners, the Friendly Society of Operative Masons proposed to abandon all initiations, oaths and regalia. They did so officially, but unofficial initiations on building scaffolds continued into the twentieth century. Andy Durr also cites the example of the way in which the legend of King Solomon's smith was still read to new members of the blacksmith's union until the late nineteenth century. A similar process of simplification and attrition of ritual is also evident in friendly societies such as the Oddfellows.

The comparisons between trade unions, friendly societies and freemasonry is not confined to the use of ritual. The importance of the tramping system has already been mentioned and it is clear that relief of this kind was available for freemasons in the early part of the nineteenth century. It would be interesting to establish how far the increasing bureaucratisation of masonic charity in England—and the development in England of such customs as the need for an invitation before visiting a lodge—were an attempt to distance freemasonry from the tramping system. Another common feature was the use of elaborate processions as the chief public face of the various associations. The importance of processions as a central function of freemasonry has now largely been forgotten, but until the 1920s, they formed a major social focus of freemasonry. Friendly society and trade union processions are better known, but trade union funerals have long been a thing of the past. In the 1830s, however, they were an important means of recruitment. One union organiser reckoned that, after a big funeral procession, recruitment could increase four-fold.

The question that remains is: were these components in early trade unions and friendly societies borrowed ultimately from freemasonry, as the Webbs believed, or did they stem from a common source? It is possible that this is a question that can never be answered. Those who have considered it hitherto have perhaps underestimated the impact of the 1799 Unlawful Societies Act on the use of ritual in friendly societies and trade unions. It is clear in the case of the Oddfellows that a great deal of their eighteenth century practices vanished after 1799. A similar process probably happened with trade unions. When ritual began to be more widely reinstated after the end of the Napoleonic Wars, it may have been necessary to develop new rituals, drawn from masonic sources. Moreover, ritual appears to have been subject to a constant process of simplification, partly as a result of the need to avoid legal difficulties. Over and above this, there would have been many complex cross-currents of borrowing and imitation, which are difficult to reconstruct. Nevertheless, I would suggest that enough survives to indicate that not all trade union ritual derives from masonic sources. The ceremonies and mythology associated with the chapels of the print shop, for example, appear to date back to at least the sixteenth century. Andy Durr prints a ritual associated with a society of horse traders which dates back perhaps to the late seventeenth century and does not seem to be derived from freemasonry.

Modern trade union historians such as Malcolm Chase and Robert Leeson, who are not subject to the same political imperatives as the Webbs, have emphasised how the roots of craft ritual probably lie quite deep. Malcolm Chase in particular has recently stated that 'the roots of trade union ritualism lay deep: it was no superficial borrowing from masonic or friendly society sources, but rather a common legacy that continued to bind all three mutualist (and still sometimes overlapping movements).' This reappraisal of the importance of ritual within the history of the trade unions reflects a reassessment by historians of the relationship between trade unionism and the associational culture of the medieval and early modern town.

At one level, the nature of the guilds and their possible links with the trade unions has been subject to radical reconsideration by historians. It has been pointed out that there are similarities of interest between guilds and early trade unions. An important preoccupation of each, for example, was the regulation of admission into apprenticeship. The old assumption that the guilds gradually faded away after the reformation has been challenged, and their flexibility and vibrancy in the sixteenth and seventeenth centuries has been emphasised. However, the guilds were subject to both internal and external pressure at this time. The reign of James II saw a complete reorganisation of the London guilds, for example, while at the same time journeymen were breaking away from the older guilds to form bodies that acted in many respects like proto-trades unions. Moreover, the highly legalistic view of guilds which was emphasised by Victorian historians who saw towns chiefly as jurisdictional units has been challenged, and replaced with a picture of guilds as just one of hundreds of different types of fraternal institutions in towns. This reassessment of the guilds has also shown how, even in the medieval period, it is not adequate to see the craft gilds as the chief associational bodies of town life—they formed part of a wide range of fraternities and clubs, which define easy categorisation.

The Webbs wrote that, where they expected to find an economic thread for a treatise, they found a spiders web. This sense of a web of associational bodies and relationships, stretching right back to the medieval period, is even stronger in modern studies of trade union history. Modern historians of trade unions emphasise continuities, but in doing so they do not suggest single lines of descent. The picture that emerges is of a wide range of associational bodies, from guilds to journeyman's clubs, box clubs and drinking clubs, overlapping and constantly generating new forms of association, from which modern trade unions gradually emerge. Raymond Postgate, in discussing the Operative Stone Masons, declared that 'Freemasonry is the legitimate child of the forbidden covines and chapters ... true operative masonry remained with the journeymen and the existing union and not the freemasonry is the real inheritor of the medieval guild'. Such attempts to establish a kind of family tree are doomed to failure in the context of the constantly fluctuating and overlapping associational world of the late medieval and early modern town.

A more fruitful approach is probably that adopted by Mary Ann Clawson in her important study of freemasonry *Constructing Brotherhood: Class, Gender and Fraternalism.* Clawson points out that journeyman's organisations, freemasonry, American labour organisations such as the Knights of Labour and even (in its earliest incarnation) the Ku Klux Klan are all types of frraternal organisation, characterised in a remarkably consistent form by a shared corporate mythology, ritual, proprietorship and masculinity. Clawson suggests that, rather than trying to trace lineal connections between these organisations, it is more appropriate to apply such sociological theories as resource mobilisation, that is, to see fraternalism as a means by which particularly groups and social classes were able to express common interests and achieve particular social aims.

Within this context, the most pressing question is perhaps not whether freemasonry, trade unions and friendly societies share common roots, but rather, how did freemasonry come to see itself as particularly distinctive and draw apart from its siblings? The process was a complex one, but one component which has been overlooked is the way in which freemasonry's successful attempts to protect itself from the effects of the legislation passed in 1799 placed it apart from friendly societies and trade unions. Although the rituals in freemasonry were subject to change, particularly at the time of the union, freemasonry remained protected from the ferocious attacks to which the ritual of trade unions and friendly societies were subject. Indeed, while the pressures on trade unions and friendly societies encouraged them to simplify their ritual, the legal protection granted to freemasonry enabled its ritual to be elaborated.

Freemasons appear actively to have supported this process of drawing apart from the unions and friendly societies in order to emphasise the respectability of their own organisation. The Duke of Sussex, in reporting his actions after the trial of the Tolpuddle Martyrs, stated that his actions were taken to defend the respectability of the craft. Shortly afterwards, a lecturer at Colchester Mechanics Institute suggested that the kind of rituals used at Tolpuddle were really no different than freemasonry. A correspondent writing to the local newspaper found this suggestion particularly offensive. The correspondent said that freemasonry was like the 'life giving sun', whereas unions were an ignis fatuus composed of noxious vapours and shining with delusive splendour. Freemasonry enshrined mortal principles; trade unions were a dangerous and destructive tendency. The suspicion of friendly societies and trade unions remained a characteristic of freemasonry. In 1829, a provincial officer wrote anxiously to the Grand Secretary asking whether it was permissible to allow an oddfellow to become a freemason, and, if a freemason became an oddfellow after his initiation, whether this prevented him from becoming a Royal Arch companion. In the 1840s, provincial officers in Wales sternly instructed freemasons to have nothing to do with such dubious bodies as the Druids and the Ivorites.

This process of suggesting that freemasonry embodied some kind of esoteric truth whereas trade union and friendly society rituals were mere mummery was, paradoxically, encouraged by radical thinkers such as Richard Carlile and his friend George Jacob Holyoake. Carlile, following Paine, saw in freemasonry forgotten remnants of ancient truths, whose true meaning he was ordained to teach to the world. By contrast, as we have seen, he strongly denounced similar rituals in trade unions and friendly societies. This kind of schizophrenia was to remain a distinctive feature of English radical thought, a tendency summed up perhaps in the figure of Annie Besant.

Somebody expressed surprise that I should be speaking on trade unions at the Canonbury Centre, whose focus is freemasonry and esotericism. But, if freemasonry has any esoteric insights to impart, it must come from its ritual, and in understanding that ritual it is essential to look at its comparators. The skeleton at Tolpuddle has as much mystical truth to impart as the temple at Great Queen Street.

A Lecture by Andrew Prescott of the Centre for Research into Freemasonry, University of Sheffield. Presented at the Canonbury Masonic Research Centre, 30 May 2001.

LODGED IN THE CANON

◆

BY S. BRENT MORRIS, Ph.D

The adventures of Mr. Sherlock Holmes as related by Dr. John H. Watson provide the reader not only with exciting tales of mystery and detection but also with a delightful glimpse into late-Victorian and early-Edwardian life in England. An important aspect of middle and upper-middle class male sociability of that era was the fraternity of Ancient Free and Accepted Masons. The Freemasons are mentioned briefly in four of the adventures, and their mention gives us some insight to the character of Holmes and Watson (and peripherally into the character of Dr. Watson's literary agent, Sir Arthur Conan Doyle).

The Masonic Fraternity

No one is quite sure of where or even when the Freemasons originated. Some have speculated they descended from the mystery religions of the Mediterranean or perhaps from the Roman College of Artificers or perhaps from the crusading Knights Templar. Most historians, however, agree that the modern social fraternity evolved during the seventeenth century from a trade organization of freemasons who met in local organizations called "lodges." The oldest Masonic document is the *Regius Poem* or *Halliwell Manuscript* of ca. 1399 in the British Museum. It is the operating rules for a trade union, with regulations for apprentices and masters, guidance for behavior, and exhortations to the members for charity and mutual support.

The oldest extant minutes of a Masonic lodge are from 1599 and belong to the Lodge of St. Mary's Chapel in Edinburgh. In those minutes a member of the lodge is reprimanded for hiring a non-Mason, that is, someone who had not gone through an apprenticeship and had been elected a member. This is exactly the behavior you would expect from a trade union. A century later in London the Freemasons are now a social fraternity, composed almost entirely of "speculative" or gentlemen Masons. In that year four of the old lodges came together to form a central authority, a "Grand Lodge," to govern the fraternity and particularly to restore the custom of the annual "Assembly and Feast."

In 1717 and before, the Masons had two levels or degrees of membership: Apprentice and Fellow-Master. Apprentices were boys or young men who served a time (usually seven years) with a Master in return for learning the trade. Upon completing an apprenticeship and satisfying a lodge of his skill, a man could be elected as a Fellow-Master in the Freemasons. Within a lodge, all Fellows were equal. A "Master" was a Fellow who was in charge of a job, supervised the work, and hired Fellows and Apprentices. About 1725 the fraternity in London introduced three-levels of membership: Apprentice, Fellowcraft, and Master. This system was eventually adopted by all lodges and is still in effect around the world today.

The Masons are famous (or possibly notorious) for their "secrets." There were, of course, the trade secrets learned by apprentices. For example, a union carpenter drives a nail with a grace and fluidity that I cannot approach, and there must have been similar trade secrets with the stonemasons. There is reason to think that some of the inner secrets of the operative masons were the geometric "secrets" of making a right angle. There were also "modes of recognition"—passwords and handshakes (called "grips") by which they can identify each other. The premier Grand Lodge was formed in 1717, and these secrets were first published in 1723 and have been in continuous print since then. They are secret only from those who do not know how to do a Google search!

These modes of recognition are thought to have originated at a time when working freemasons needed a means to identify themselves as a lodge member when they travelled from one job site to another. Unlike members of other trades—bakers, carpenters, or tailors, for example—freemasons might not always have work in one location. When a town's bridge or church was completed, there might not be more work for decades within that community. Thus the necessity for masons to travel arose, and soon thereafter came the requirement of some way for a travelling mason to identify himself at a new job site, if the integrity of the trade organization and its training were to be maintained.

This system of symbolic "secret knowledge" has been maintained for centuries, and even today a visiting Mason before gaining admission to a lodge must prove himself knowledgeable in the "secrets of Masonry." Since the Masons' secrets have been long-published, one may well ask the question, "What's the point?" Today the secrets are purely symbolic, a token of a Mason's integrity and his fidelity to his trust.

After Freemasonry emerged in early eighteenth-century Britain, it migrated around the globe and found fertile soil in most European countries and their colonies. Other countries grafted additional levels of membership or degrees onto the original and universal three from England. A Masonic degree is a brief morality play or ceremony that teaches a lesson such as fidelity, truth, benevolence, and so on. The Scottish Rite, which originated in France, has thirty-three degrees; the York Rite, which originated in America, has twelve degrees; the Rite of Memphis, which originated in Italy, has over ninety degrees; and the Swedish Rite, which originated in Sweden, has eleven degrees.

Freemasonry in Victorian England

When Queen Victoria ascended to the throne in 1837, Freemasonry had become part of the accepted social activities for a gentleman. A place to gather with friends where rank and station meant much less than on the outside. The Duke of Sussex was Grand Master of England in 1837, and his participation represented the general approbation given the fraternity. Victoria's son, Albert Edward, later served as Grand Master when he was Prince of Wales, and when he ascended the throne as Edward VII, he was succeeded as Grand Master by his brother, the Duke of Connaught. As an indication of the wide spread nature of English Freemasonry, the 2,076th English lodge, Quatuor Coronati, was chartered in 1884.

Sir Charles Warren, an explorer and archaeologist, was the first Master of Quatuor Coronati, a lodge devoted to the history of Freemasonry and limited to no more than forty members at any time. Their annual transactions, *Ars Quatuor Coronatorum*, have been published since 1885 and could be called the *Baker Street Journal* of Freemasonry. Sir Charles served as Metropolitan Police Commissioner from March 1886 to November 1887 during the Jack the Ripper murders. Stephen Knight latched upon the Masonic membership of Warren and built it into a complex Masonic conspiracy to explain the Ripper murders that was published in *Jack the Ripper: The Final Solution*. Knight's fantasy in turn served as the basis of the 1980 pastiche movie, *Murder by Decree*, in which Sir Charles Warren "is confronted by Sherlock Holmes who claims special knowledge of The Royal Order of Freemasons giving him some strange and curious signs and identifying Sir Charles as a 33rd Degree Mason by the insignia on his ring. (Sir Charles, in fact, only reached the 30th Degree....)"[1]

Other prominent Victorian-era Masons include Sir Arthur S. Sullivan, the composer, Sir William S. Gilbert, the librettist, Anthony Trollope, the author,

Rudyard Kipling, the author, Frédéric August Bartholdi, the designer of the Statue of Liberty, Sir Richard Francis Burton, the explorer and translator of *The Arabian Nights*, Mark Twain, the author, Alphonse Mucha, the Czech artist, Harry Houdini, the magician and anti-spiritualist crusader, and Sir Arthur Conan Doyle, the author and spiritualist.

Freemasonry in the Canon

Freemasonry is mentioned briefly in only four adventures, but it is possible to make a few tentative deductions from them. Let us consider each in turn.

A Study in Scarlet. As Sherlock Holmes investigates the murder of Enoch Drebber, he asks Inspector Tobias Gregson, "What did you find in the pockets?" Among the items Gregson listed from Drebber was a "gold ring, with Masonic device." The device was probably the well known square and compasses, and as Drebber was American, there was most likely a letter "G" in the center of the tools, standing for both *geometry* and *God*. British and European Masons usually don't use the "G."

Drebber was a member of the Church of Jesus Christ of Latter Day Saints, the Mormons. The Prophet Joseph Smith was a Mason and helped initiate over 1,000 Mormons in Nauvoo, Illinois, where he was eventually murdered while being held in the Nauvoo jail. His brother Hyrum and Brigham Young were also Masons, so it would not be surprising to find an early Mormon who was a Mason, even though later events soured relations between the LDS Church and Freemasonry for decades.

A Scandal in Bohemia. Sherlock Holmes watched the habits and the house of Miss Irene Adler while disguised as a horse groom. He says to Watson, "There is a wonderful sympathy and freemasonry among horsy men. Be one of them, and you will know all there is to know." We can deduce little special about Holmes use of the term, which emphasizes the well known closeness and friendliness of the fraternity.

The Adventure of the Retired Colourman. Holmes sends Watson to gather information on Josiah Amberly, a retired manufacturer of artists' supplies. When Watson reports back, he says that he thinks he was followed by a "tall, dark" man. Holmes adds, before Watson can say so, that the man was mustached, wore

---

1.   Yasha Beresiner, "Arthur Conan Doyle: Spiritualist and Freemason," Pietre-Stones Review of Freemasonry, www.freemasons-freemasonry.com/beresiner10.html, accessed March 8, 2006.

dark glasses, and a Masonic tie-pin. This turns out to be Mr. Barker, and nothing else is said about his Masonic jewelry.

The Red-Headed League. When Sherlock Holmes first meets Jabez Wilson, he says, "Beyond the obvious facts that he has at some time done manual labour, that he takes snuff, that he is a Freemason, that he has been in China, and that he has done a considerable amount of writing lately, I can deduce nothing more." When Wilson presses him on how he knew he was a Freemason, Holmes says, "I won't insult your intelligence by telling you how I read that, especially as, rather against the strict rules of your order, you use an arc and compass breast pin." Because Jabez Wilson was a client and needed a demonstration of Holmes' techniques, he was identified as a Mason and then politely reprimanded. Mr. Barker, Holmes' "hated rival upon the Surrey shore," on the other hand, needed no such demonstration and did not receive a reprimand. In fact, it was Watson who observed the Masonic pin, and Holmes deduced its presence from previous experience with Barker.

Holmes' statement indicates remarkable knowledge about the customs of the fraternity. Since the late 1700s British and American applicants for Masonic membership must declare in writing that "Unbiased by friends and uninfluenced by mercenary motives, I freely and voluntarily offer myself a candidate for the mysteries of masonry."[2] There is no formal rule against English Masons wearing Masonic jewelry, but it has been discouraged within their lodges since the late 1800s. "English Masons are exhorted not to misuse their membership [for personal gain] and the wearing of such jewelry may be misconstrued as a discreet advertisement thereof for improper purposes."[3] This is not secret or even private information, but it is certainly something that wouldn't be known from a casual study of the fraternity.

Wilson wore an "arc and compass breast pin," not the much more common square and compass. Since 1814 in England, the arc or protractor and compass has been the emblem of a Past Grand Master. The pin is rarely seen since English Grand Masters usually serve for 20–30 years, and they have been selected from the nobility for nearly 300 years. However, in the United States the arc and compass pin is the most common emblem of a Past Master of a lodge. With thousands of lodges generating a new Past Master each year, such a pin is not uncommon.

---

2.   William Preston, *Illustrations of Free-Masonry* (London: The Author, 1772), pp. 210–11.

3.   Robert T. Runciman, "Sir Arthur Conan Doyle, Sherlock Holmes, and Freemasonry," *Ars Quatuor Coronatorum*, vol. 104 (1991), pp. 178–87.

The mystery then is not how Sherlock Holmes identified the pin, for surely a man who studied cigar ashes would be familiar with the identifying jewelry of all sorts of organizations. Rather, the mystery is how Jabez Wilson came to have such a pin. A quick check of a list of English Past Grand Masters reveals that Jabez Wilson's name is conspicuous for its absence. Perhaps in his travels he resided long enough in America to affiliate with a lodge and become its Past Master. It is more likely that he came across the pin in a pawn shop for a good price. If Wilson were a casual Mason, one who joined to rub shoulders with those he considered to be above his station, then he might not have appreciated the subtle distinction between the arc and square in the pin, and snatched it up for his personal and incorrect use.

The Adventure of the Norwood Builder. The "unhappy John Hector McFarlane" presents himself to Holmes as a client and is told, "Beyond the obvious facts that you are a bachelor, a solicitor, a Freemason, and an asthmatic, I know nothing whatever about you." Watson was able to follow these deductions and in particular observed McFarlane's watch-charm. We are not told which of several Masonic emblems was on the charm, but it gave away his Masonic membership.

Our attention is drawn to the curious incident of the watch-charm on the client. Holmes said nothing to his client about wearing such jewelry as he did to Jabez Wilson. That is the curious incident.

Here again we see Holmes remarkable knowledge of the fraternity. McFarlane's name indicates Scots descent. Cecil A. Ryder observed in "A Study in Masonry," that McFarlane "would probably have received his Masonic degrees in Scotland. It is not unusual for Scots Masons, who are not forbidden to do so, to wear the insignia."[4]

The Source of Holmes' Masonic Knowledge

The superficial conclusion is that Sherlock Holmes was a Freemason, given his detailed knowledge of the fraternity. This deduction flies in the face of what we know about Holmes as a social creature. While not lacking in social graces, the great detective did not seek out human companionship or maintain close friendships, except perhaps with Dr. Watson. In contrast a Masonic lodge is a celebration of sociability and friendship, a place where men gather for the purpose of enjoying each other's company. It would be fair to describe a Masonic lodge as an "Anti-Diogenes Club," and this does not seem the sort of organization that

---

4.   Cecil A. Ryder quoted in Runciman, p. 185.

would be attractive to Sherlock Holmes. Further, recall that Holmes tells Jabez Wilson, that wearing an arc and compass breast pin is "rather against the strict rules of *your* order." Had Holmes been a Mason, he would have referred to "*our* order."

I believe that the source of Holmes' familiarity with Masonic customs came from his chronicler, John H. Watson, M.D. As a veteran, Watson would have enjoyed the male-bonding experiences of the army. His outgoing and sociable nature would have fit naturally into a Masonic lodge. In his many discussions with Holmes, it would have been natural and not at all improper to explain the subtleties of Masonic jewelry and the different customs between English and Scots and other Masons.

Now, we must ask, was Watson an active Mason. The absence of any other mention of the fraternity in the Canon would indicate that Watson was very discrete about his membership, perhaps not wanting to use it for personal gain by attracting readers who might not have otherwise been interested in his writing. Watson would have preferred his literary efforts to stand or fall on their own merits. Of course the evidence could also support the contention that Watson was inactive, perhaps because of the pressures of his medical practice or because the fraternity did not meet his needs.

It is illustrative if we compare Watson's career to a contemporary medical and literary colleague, Sir Arthur Conan Doyle. Dr. Doyle joined Phoenix Lodge No. 257 in 1887 and withdrew his membership only two years later in 1889. He remained unaffiliated and inactive until 1901 when the Lodge of St. Mary's Chapel in Edinburgh invited him to a meeting to give a toast to the "Immortal Memory of Queen Victoria," and they afterwards made him an honorary member. Doyle rejoined Phoenix lodge in 1902, but withdrew again in 1911. There is no evidence that he every participated after that.

Some insight to Doyle's disaffection with Freemasonry can be found in one of his Professor Challenger stories, *The Land of Mist.* A character is described as "a pompous ass named Weatherby. He is one of those who wander about on the obscure edges of Masonry, talking with whispers and reverence on mysteries where no mystery is. Spiritualism, with its very real and awful mysteries, is, to him, a vulgar thing because it brought consolation to common folk."[5]

We can understand the Masonic references lodged in the Canon with the simple insight that John H. Watson was a Freemason. Like his fellow author of that period, Arthur Conan Doyle, Watson apparently found that the fraternity did

---

5.   Beresiner, "Arthur Conan Doyle."

not satisfy his needs as he had hoped, and so he became inactive. But even if he withdrew his membership from his lodge, I am confident that he never forgot the principal teachings of Brotherly Love, Relief, and Truth.